A PARENT'S WORKBOOK 1:

SEARCHING, DISCUSSING AND STUDYING SCRIPTURES

By

Teresa Billingsley

ISBN: 978-1-946662-01-9

Disclaimer

"*A Parent's Workbook 1: Searching, Discussing & Studying Scriptures*" was written to provide accurate and current information for those who either are raising a teenager, or are considering being a positive influence on youth in today's society. It is not intended to substitute for personal advice from a sound spiritual or parental leader. If you have any immediate questions or matters, and you need one-on-one counseling to address your specific situation, I encourage you to seek out the services of a qualified licensed professional in your area to address your particular issues and concerns.

The opinions expressed in this book are those of the author's and should not be construed as representing the opinions of any particular group, religion or translation of The Bible. It is recommended that you read the relevant scriptures cited for clarification.

Dedication

I dedicate this book to my lord and savior, Jesus Christ, first and foremost. Second, in honor of introducing me to the scriptures and living a godly life in front of me, I pay homage to my mother (Bertha Billingsley) as well. Finally, to the parents, communities, relatives, youth groups, volunteers and ministries who strives to find ways to bridge the gap between parents and teens, I wrote this book for you and with you in mind.

Acknowledgement

I am grateful for the word of God. It provides sustenance and guidance in every aspect of life. I strongly recommend The Bible as the primary source of sound counsel. If you are open and receptive to it, you will gain knowledge and wisdom for all that ails you.

I urge anyone interested in making your relationship with youth the best it could possibly be to research the scriptures. Also, humbly learn from both mature and baby Christians who search the word, speak the truth in love and who will cover you in prayer.

Introduction

To maximize the benefits and educational value of this study you should have first completed my online courses, "Anger Management" and "4 Personality Types." If you have not experienced these courses, then certain questions in this book may be difficult to answer and expound on. Some of the terms and personality types may be foreign to you. However, the scriptures are still relevant and captivating enough to provide you with an array of topics to create some great discussions.

You are not constrained to my questions. They may assist you in coming up with your own that you find more relevant to your family and problems you may currently be facing.

My primary goal is to do one thing. I want to inspire you to hunger after a relationship with God. I would like to wet the palate of youth to cause them to thirst after the word of God and want to search the scriptures. I personally do not have all the answers and I am constantly evolving and continue to be a work in progress.

A few things I have found and am convinced about is God is real, The Bible is true and I personally need God's guidance on a daily basis. My body, mind and spirit gets fed every day. What I feed it grows in me and gets stronger. I can either allow the junk of the world to feed me and let that grow, or I can make a conscious decision to feed it with the word of God and let good things grow in me. The choice is mine.

If I do nothing, then my decision is to let the world dictate right and wrong. The alternative requires effort to become enlightened so I can know how to live a life on purpose and complete the assignment I was born to do. If you too are interested in the latter, enlightenment, purpose and growth then this material will be helpful to you.

Table of Contents

Questions

Instructions

You are given a segment of the Bible to read and a list of questions. The questions prevent you from simply scanning the text and cause you to study it. There is a reason why you are asked to summarize what you read and then write down what you got out of the scriptures. There will be a slight twist and variation for everyone.

If you were not asked to do this and chose to discuss it in an open forum, the temptation will be for you to follow suit and piggyback off the first and most vocal person who shares their perspective. You may think your own point of view is incorrect or insignificant. The truth is, your revelation is equally important and needs to be shared too.

One of the wonderful and exciting things about the word of God is that it can speak directly to you and me and touch on our individual situations like nothing else written. I want you to be sure not to discount what you got out of your study time and the messages spoken to *your* heart. Expect it to be different as well as similar to what was revealed to others. The more open you are the more apt you are to receive answers and revelations that will amaze you.

Try not to get hung up on my answers or the answers of others. The scriptures were written long ago, I did not write them and do not claim to have license to interpret them for you. I provided questions and answers to these questions. If my answers are based on a verse, I indicate the verse or verses that I base my answer on. You may get a different answer or interpretation, that is perfectly fine. Just articulate your understanding and what scriptures you base your answers on.

I love the word of God and I enjoy fellowshipping and discussing it with others who have a genuine desire to build or strengthen their relationship with God. I do not argue over scripture nor put my opinion above others. I personally do not believe the scriptures were written to incite contention or confusion. Nor do I ascribe to the belief that the scriptures are to be used as a weapon against a fellow believer. I see The Bible as our instruction manual to empower and equip us to live our lives with divine purpose. I implore you to utilize the material to grow. Adapt it and introduce it to teens as productive exercises.

Adam and Eve

I.   The assigned reading for this bible study is <u>Genesis 2-3</u>

II.   Once you have finished reading the above listed passages of scripture answer the two below questions:

1. Sum up this reading assignment in 50 words or less. Let others know and remind yourself what this segment was about:

2. What did you learn from reading these scriptures that relate to what you are currently dealing with?

- ____
- ____
- ____
- ____
- ____
- ____

- _______________________________
  ____
- _______________________________
  ____
- _______________________________
  ____
- _______________________________
  ____

III.   What new insight did you gain from discussing this with others? What did they help you see in the passage that you overlooked and can apply in your daily living? What unique perspective did someone else add that you found beneficial?

Adam & Eve – Genesis 2-3

Read Genesis 2-3 to assist you in answering the below questions.

Questions & Answers:

Genesis 2
1. Which day did God bless and sanctify?
2. What did the scripture say God did immediately thereafter?
3. What do you do on the Sabbath?
4. What day of the week is your Sabbath day, if you have one?
5. What weather condition do we experience today that had not happened yet?
6. What was formed from dust?
7. What happened that caused what was formed to breathe and come to life?
8. Who made every tree?
9. How were the trees described?
10. What were the two distinctions between trees?
11. What is the name of the second river?
12. What land does this river surround/encompass?
13. What reason did God put man in the garden?

14. What is another way of describing the reason God put man in the garden?
15. What freedom did God give Adam concerning the trees?
16. What one boundary or restriction did God give Adam concerning the trees?
17. What was he told would happen if the man broke this rule?
18. Is it important to have boundaries? Explain
19. List at least 3 freedoms or blessings your parents have given you:
20. List at least 3 boundaries your parents have for you:
21. What was it God said was not good about man's circumstances?
22. What did God decide was the solution?
23. What was the problem God had with naming the creatures?
24. What did God cause to happen to Adam?
25. Briefly describe the first reported surgery and who performed it:
26. What did God make during this procedure?
27. How was this gift God made Adam introduced?
28. What did Adam say that let us know he recognized she was a part of him?
29. Who named her and what was she named?
30. What is the reason a man should leave his father and mother?
31. What condition were they in that may cause others to be embarrassed or ashamed?
32. Describe a situation where you were not ashamed until someone said something to you?

Genesis 3
1. What was the shrewdest and most subtle beast of the field?
2. How was this beast made?

3. What unique abilities did this beast have that it no longer has?
4. What was the first thing this beast challenged?
5. Who do you allow to speak to you and influence your decisions?
6. Why was the serpent making this his business? Why was he asking about what *they* could do and eat?
7. Have you ever had others question you about the rules your parents gave you? Explain
8. What are some counterpunches you could use in the future?
9. Do you think others are asking questions to help you obey?
10. What are some good solutions to avoid being tricked and manipulated by others to break the rules?
11. What were the biggest mistakes these two made?
12. What did she say God's boundary was regarding what they could eat?
13. Did the woman relay God's rule correctly or add or delete instructions? Explain
14. What rules have you misinterpreted or altered in the past so you could do what you wanted?
15. What laws or rules in society do you see being modified and misconstrued so people can sin? Explain
16. Would it have been easier to have the rule in writing to refer to?
17. Still today people are more trusting with their friends and family. They choose to make verbal arrangements and not put their agreement in writing. Is this wise? Explain
18. What does the serpent's behavior tell you about outsiders who have an opinion or curiosity about rules your parents have given you for your own good?
19. Do you think having the rules in writing prevents people from doing the wrong thing?

20. What purpose is there for having rules or agreements in writing? Does it make a difference? Explain

21. The serpent said, "You won't die." Why should this have been the biggest red flag to stop talking and listening to the serpent?

22. The serpent said, "Because God knows if you eat you'll be like him, your mind will be opened and you'll know good from evil." Some of what the serpent said was true but it was twisted truth. Explain

23. Do you know of other promotions or commercials, that only give partial or misleading endorsements promoting heavenly results without telling you the true cost and side effects? Give some examples:

24. What lies and negative self-talk comes to your mind that make you question your parent's rules?

25. What is a good counterpunch to use when someone is telling you God's rules will ruin your fun?

26. We have decided as a society youth do not have the brain development and authority to make certain decisions until 18 years of age. Is this meant to protect youth or hurt youth? Explain

27. It is hard to retain knowledge, understanding and rules that is why it is important for adults to find ways of reminding you constantly in order for you to automatically react properly. Without practice and repetition, you are prone to forget the rules and boundaries God and society have set. What examples can you list of things or routines that are taught to indoctrinate youth of beliefs and rules?

28. Have there been any rulers, leaders, or presidents who have used the youth as a tool to divide the family? Explain

29. Before we sin or are disobedient, often one or more of our 5 senses engages our mind to create a convincing self-dialogue for us to act. What are the 5 senses?
30. Can you see why food is such a huge temptation in the Bible and in life? Explain how it engages our senses:
31. What excuses do you think were being played in their heads to prompt Adam and Eve to sin?
32. Which of the five senses got the woman's attention? Explain
33. Why did she desire the tree, what did she think it could do for her?
34. What did she do next and who did she involve?
35. What do you think came to mind when each one was called out on their own sin?
36. What did sin and disobedience do to this couple and forever change?
37. Sin can prematurely open your eyes to evil and upset your spirit and your conscience. Name some temptations people fall for listening to the media, peers, and others. Also, list some of the consequences that result that you don't find out about unless you fall prey to the temptation of sin?
38. What are some counterpunches you could use in the future if someone is trying to persuade you to disregard your parent's instructions and God's laws?
39. It is said that sin causes a divide and separation from God. Is this demonstrated in this chapter? After Adam and the woman sinned, describe their next interaction with God:
40. Do you know how Adam and Eve felt? Have you ever sinned against God and decided to avoid the church, your parents or other Christians? Explain
41. Have you ever been involved in doing something your parents have told you not to do, and been startled by their voice calling you or them calling your phone? Have you

found yourself avoiding them, hiding, or having a strained conversation to hide what you have done or were about to do? Explain

42. What did God ask Adam?

43. What do you think the significance was in God asking Adam this question, we know God knew the answer to?

44. What was Adam's answer to the question God asked?

45. Why do you think Adam's response hurt him rather than help him?

46. What did Adam's answer to God reveal?

47. What were the next two questions God asked Adam?

48. When you disobey your parents and let someone evil speak in your ear to you, what is bound to occur?

49. Did Adam take responsibility for what he did? If he didn't own up to his part, who did Adam blame?

50. What did the Lord ask the woman?

51. What did the woman answer?

52. Did the woman accept responsibility for what she did or blame others?

53. Who is responsible for what you do?

54. Is it an excuse if someone tells you to do something your parents have told you not to do? Explain

55. Did God reprimand anyone else other than Adam and the woman? Explain

56. What was the serpent's curse/punishment?

57. Based on the serpent's punishment/curse, what may that mean as to how he was formed prior?

58. What else is different about the serpent then and now?

59. What else can we learn from the interaction between the serpent, Adam and the woman?

60. Before you judge Adam and the woman, ask yourself, "What am I currently allowing to tell me what to do, that I have dominion over?
61. Is the woman's seed/offspring and the serpent's seed/offspring enemies?
62. What was the woman's curse?
63. The woman's punishment was to have great sorrow during what times?
64. What did God say Adam did wrong?
65. What consequences resulted from Adam's mistakes?
66. What did God curse?
67. What must he do all the days of his life?
68. What were they destined to eat?
69. What were they now required to do the remainder of their lives to eat
70. What was Adam told he was made of and would eventually return to?
71. What did Adam rename the woman?
72. What did her name mean?
73. What was made for Adam and his wife to clothe them?
74. Who made it?
75. The Lord God proclaimed that Adam now had what newfound knowledge?
76. How long would man live if he ate from the tree of life?
77. What were they banished from the garden of Eden to do?
78. What beings were placed east of Eden?
79. What object was turned every way to keep and guard the way of the tree of life?

Extra Credit Questions:

80. What did Adam and the woman eat that Adam was told not to eat? What scripture(s) support and confirm your answer?
81. If I were to ask most ministers and most people, the prior question (#80) what answer would they give me?
82. Why is it important to get our answers and wisdom from scriptures?

TERESA BILLINGSLEY

NOTES

The Temptation of Jesus

I.   The assigned reading for this bible study is <u>Matthew 4:1-11</u>

II.   Once you have finished reading the above listed passages of scripture answer the two below questions:

1.   Sum up this reading assignment in 50 words or less. Let others know and remind yourself what this segment was about:

2.   What did you learn from reading these scriptures that relate to what you are currently dealing with?

-
-
-
-
-
-
-

- ______________________________________

- ______________________________________

- ______________________________________

- ______________________________________

III.   What new insight did you gain from discussing this with others? What did they help you see in the passage that you overlooked and can apply in your daily living? What unique perspective did someone else add that you found beneficial?

The Temptation of Jesus – Matthew 4:1-11

Please read Matthew 4:1-11 for the answers to the questions below.

Questions

1. Who or what led Jesus into the wilderness?
2. Who or what was going to tempt Jesus?
3. What did Jesus do that caused him to be hungry?
4. How long did he do this?
5. What was the very first 7 words the tempter said to Jesus?
6. Why is this important?
7. Have you ever gotten angry because someone called you out of your name?
8. What difference does it make if others fail to know or acknowledge who you are, as long as the people who matter know you?
9. What did the tempter tell Jesus to do to prove who Jesus was?
10. Have you ever been told to do something or challenged to prove something to others?
11. What was Jesus' response?

12. What did Jesus' response mean?
13. Where was Jesus taken next?
14. Who took him there?
15. Where was Jesus put?
16. This time what was the first 7 words said to Jesus?
17. What was Jesus told to do to prove himself this time?
18. What 3 words did the devil use to support his position?
19. Why are these three words so important?
20. What protection was Jesus told he had?
21. List some examples of assurances instigators give people that are unreliable?
22. What initial words did Jesus say in response?
23. What did Jesus say about temptation?
24. What did Jesus mean by this?
25. Where was Jesus taken next, and by who?
26. What was he shown?
27. Jesus was offered these things if Jesus agreed to do what?
28. What did Jesus say in response?
29. What did the devil do next?
30. What positive thing occurred in the end?
31. What does this passage of scripture demonstrate to you?
32. If Jesus had become violent or enraged at having one challenge back to back, do you think he would have had the same outcome? Explain

NOTES

Bad News

I.   The assigned reading for this bible study is <u>Matthew 4:12-17</u>

II.   Once you have finished reading the above listed passages of scripture answer the two below questions:

1. Sum up this reading assignment in 50 words or less. Let others know and remind yourself what this segment was about:

2. What did you learn from reading these scriptures that relate to what you are currently dealing with?

- ____

- ____

- ____

- ____

- ____

- ____

- _______________________________
  ____
- _______________________________
  ____
- _______________________________
  ____
- _______________________________
  ____

III.   What new insight did you gain from discussing this with others? What did they help you see in the passage that you overlooked and can apply in your daily living? What unique perspective did someone else add that you found beneficial?

Bad News – Matthew 4:12-17

*~ You should have already read Matthew 4:1-11 and
completed the lesson, Jesus Tempted ~*

1. What happened before this next reading assignment?

Read Matthew 4:12-17 to answer the following questions:

2. Jesus receives news, what was he told?
3. He left what place to go where?
4. Did he go to see John, protest, or get him out of prison? Explain
5. What untrue criticisms do you think friends, family and others would later say about Jesus for doing this?
6. Do you think anyone understood at the time why Jesus did not immediately go to John's defense? Explain
7. What can Christ's response teach you?
8. Have you ever been in a situation where what you knew was the right thing to do was guaranteed to attract criticism from strangers and those close to you? Explain
9. Knowing what we know now, if you had an opportunity to encourage Jesus at this beginning stage, what would you have said to him?

10. Was Jesus conscious of living a life on purpose and not acting on his own? Explain
11. What was the prophesy spoken and who spoke it?
12. Because of his obedience, what began to happen for Jesus next?
13. What was his first recorded message centered around?
14. What does Christ's message mean to you?

Extra credit questions (The answers are not found in Matthew 4):

15. What scriptures in The Bible address the timing of the enemy's attacks on our lives?

16. Every stage of life is important and a part of life. List the scriptures that tell us trials and temptations are not strange _(A)_ nor uncommon _(B)_. We can rest in knowing that we can endure troubles because of the joy of the anticipated end result _(C)_.

17. This lesson is a reminder of what?

NOTES

Esther

I.   The assigned reading for this bible study is <u>Esther 1-10</u>

II.   Once you have finished reading the above listed passages of scripture answer the two below questions:

1. Sum up this reading assignment in 50 words or less. Let others know and remind yourself what this segment was about:

2. What did you learn from reading these scriptures that relate to what you are currently dealing with?

- ____
- ____
- ____
- ____
- ____
- ____

- _______________________________

- _______________________________

- _______________________________

- _______________________________

III.　　What new insight did you gain from discussing this with others? What did they help you see in the passage that you overlooked and can apply in your daily living? What unique perspective did someone else add that you found beneficial?

Esther – Chapters 1-10

Read Esther 1-10 to assist you in answering the below questions.

Questions

Esther 1

1. What was the limit the king placed on wine consumption?
2. What was the first law, rule or stipulation mentioned in Esther 1?
3. Is it a good idea for people to decide to consume as much alcohol as they want? Explain
4. If you were having a party at your home would you have this same rule? What if you had a job as a judge or well-known political leader that came with a lot of responsibility and public/civic recognition?
5. The king was intoxicated, is this appropriate behavior for a king?
6. What scriptures in The Bible address intoxication and whether a king or leader should drink or be intoxicated?
7. Why was the king calling for Queen Vashti?

8. Did his staff do the right thing in carrying out the king's request, or should they have tried to talk him out of it?
9. Did Queen Vashti do the right thing, or should she have handled it differently?
10. If you were Queen Vashti, what would you have done?
11. Is this the kind of behavior of a male who cares about a female, or is this the behavior of a drunk male showing off?
12. What was the king's response?
13. Did the king have a right to be angry? Explain
14. Do you think this would have happened if the king had been sober? Explain
15. Do people normally make better decisions the more alcohol they consume or the soberer they are?
16. Were there any anger symptoms listed that should have given the king warning to reverse the symptoms?
17. Did the king immediately react pleased with Queen Vashti?
18. Should the king have immediately responded?
19. Does this king sound like a bad or violent man? Explain
20. Why do you think he consulted advisers and not strangers, friends or relatives?
21. What was the king's intent for contacting advisers?
22. What was the expertise of the advisers the king consulted?
23. Was Memucan's advice given in the best interest of the people or self-serving? What should this teach you to be cautious of?
24. What dangerous distorted thinking and anger pattern were being promoted in verse 18?
25. Does putting a rule in writing and making it into law change a person's rebellious heart?
26. Was this thought out enough and with the right people deciding whether it should become a law or not?

27. Do you think the king took Memucan's suggestion because he was offended or because he thought it would help strengthen couples' relationships?
28. What did the king do to make sure everyone was made aware of this new law?
29. The rule to let guests be carefree and drink as much as they want are characteristics of what personality type?
30. When king Ahasuerus went to his advisers and wanted to punish Vashti within their law, this is a characteristic of what personality type?

Esther 2

1. Verse 1 says the king cooled off and remembered what Vashti did and what he decreed against her. What does this tell us about his rationale before?
2. Why were virgins preferred to be the king's wife?
3. Did the king like Esther?
4. Was she liked any more than other women by the king? How do you know?
5. What advice did Mordecai give Esther? Why?
6. If you were given this same advice would it upset you? Explain
7. Have you ever been told this before, to deny a part of who you are? If you answered yes, how did it make you feel?
8. Why do you think Mordecai told Esther to keep this information about herself private?
9. What plot did Mordecai find out about? What if anything did he do about it?
10. Did anyone else do anything about this information Mordecai had?

11. If you were Mordecai would you have done or said anything or just acted like you knew nothing?

Esther 3

1. The king's servants manipulated Haman much like instigators manipulate two people into fights. Explain.
2. Was Haman angry with Mordecai before these servants spoke to him?
3. Should you beware of anyone coming to you and pointing out someone alleged to have disrespected you to your face repeatedly that you did not notice?
4. Why do you think these servants told Haman about Mordecai?
5. Could these servants possibly be jealous and upset with Haman about his promotion?
6. Why was it important to note that when they found out Mordecai was a Jew the servants decided to report him?
7. Now Haman noticed Mordecai didn't bow or reverence him and Haman was happy right?
8. Mordecai had been doing this and Haman was unaffected so it wasn't the event, what changed?
9. How do you think the servants characterized Mordecai to Haman to get this new response?
10. Did Haman want to punish just Mordecai?
11. Haman's anger was magnification and escalating in what way?
12. What did Haman recommend to the king because he was offended by Mordecai?
13. If you not only suggest a plan but provide funding to legislate it does this make those in authority pay attention?

14. Was Haman known to have a good relationship with all races?
15. When the king gave Haman his ring, was this a good move because he could trust Haman to act fairly?
16. Did the king give any special instruction to Haman not to abuse his authority?
17. When if at all did Haman have an order written into law?
18. What was the consequence if any for defying the new law?
19. Was there a reward / incentive for reporting violators? If your answer is yes, what was it?
20. Do you think offering a reward or incentive would inspire people who may not normally want to act?
21. Who if anyone would be punished?
22. What had to happen before people were ready to act?
23. Once the decree went out what was the king and Haman's reaction?
24. What was the reaction of the people in the city?

Esther 4

1. How did Mordecai react when he found out about the new law?
2. Was Mordecai's dramatic response in compliance with their laws and customs?
3. If you act in compliance to a written law in your jurisdiction, is that enough to justify your actions?
4. Was Mordecai's anger needless? Explain
5. Was Mordecai's anger just? Explain
6. Was Mordecai's anger causing a problem? Explain
7. How did the Jews respond?
8. Esther sent Mordecai clothing when she found out he was protesting. Was he grateful? Why or why not?

9. Did Esther send a messenger to arrest Mordecai and have him locked up?
10. Where was Mordecai protesting? Why do you think he chose this location?
11. Being seen and heard are character traits of what personality type?
12. Did the manner in which Mordecai chose to protest help or hurt his cause?
13. Would you protest the same way Mordecai did if it were legal?
14. What is the point of protesting?
15. How do you respond to authority figures and institutions when you feel their actions are adversely unfair?
16. Mordecai responded and answered the question what was wrong. He didn't just ask that his word be taken as proof, what else did Mordecai do that helped his position?
17. Who did Mordecai ask and depend on to do something about the problem?
18. Should Mordecai have waited until he had organized a large group of supporters before acting?
19. If you were Esther would you jeopardize your life and status to jump into this fight? Why or why not?
20. Esther had a good reason not to approach the king, what was it?
21. Is it important to know the law when you want to fight something you perceive as an injustice? Explain
22. What arguments were given to Esther if she did nothing?
23. List some things trend setters, freedom fighters, and advocates must be willing to do to try to reverse injustice:
24. Is it important to have faith and a spiritual foundation to reflect on? Explain

25. What five words are Esther famous for saying regarding how much she was willing to sacrifice?
26. What is Mordecai's famous saying to Esther regarding her purpose in life?
27. What did Esther ask Mordecai to do?
28. Did Mordecai comply?
29. Often people ask you to take and put yourself at risk but are not willing to do anything themselves, true or false?

Esther 5

1. Did Esther approach the king wisely or recklessly?
2. Did the king have the same regard for Esther that he had for Queen Vashti? Explain
3. Was Queen Esther and Queen Vashti regarded by king Ahasuerus the same? Explain
4. What promise did the king make to Queen Esther?
5. When a king made a vow or public promise could he later change his mind? Explain
6. What other stories in the Bible do you know of where kings made a law or promise and wished they had not?
7. How much was the king willing to grant Esther?
8. King Ahasuerus' willingness to grant Esther whatever she wanted without knowing what she would ask for says what about his views and feelings for her?
9. Have you built the kind of relationship with your parents where you can garner the same response from them that the king gave Esther? Explain ways you can do this:
10. The king obligated Haman to attend Esther's banquet, why?
11. Have you earned the kind of trust and respect the king had for Esther? Explain

12. Are your requests met with many questions to determine your agenda or what you are choosing not to tell your parents? Explain
13. Or are your parent's eager to give you any requests you make because you have lived a responsible honest life thus far? Explain
14. Are there changes you can make to rebuild trust and earn your parents respect? List them:
15. Have you ever let your parents down after they trusted you with permission to do something?
16. Was it a big deal for the king to be willing to grant Esther an unknown request? Explain
17. Have you taken your parent's permission for granted in the past? Will you correct that now?
18. Even after being granted anything she wished, Esther responded humble and gracious. Explain
19. Haman felt good about himself after receiving the invitation until what happened?
20. Was Haman's anger needless? Explain
21. Was Haman's anger just? Explain
22. Did the act/event justify the level of Haman's anger? Explain
23. What did Haman decide to do about his anger? Why?
24. Was Haman a humble guy? Explain
25. Did Haman have anything to be thankful for?
26. With all that Haman had, how did he let his anger cause him to focus on an encounter that upset him?
27. When Haman was boasting do you think this was helping him win friends or causing people to be jealous of him and not like him?
28. Do jealous people wait for an opportunity to bring you down or lift you up?

29. Have you ever had an experience with a jealous person who was upset with you? Tell me about it
30. What was Haman's wife's name?
31. Haman's wife suggested Haman ask the king for permission to hang Mordecai. Does she sound like a good person to be around and influencing Haman?
32. Who have you been around who is like Haman's wife?
33. What did Haman think of his wife's idea?

Esther 6

1. When the king could not sleep what did he decide to do?
2. When you are bored and can't sleep what do you do with your time?
3. What did the king uncover?
4. Was the king angry after finding out this new information? If not, what was his response?
5. Who did the king uncover information about?
6. Who showed up in the king's outward court?
7. What did this person want?
8. What did the king ask Haman's opinion on?
9. Did Haman give the king good advice?
10. Why do you think he gave the advice he did?
11. Did the king like Haman's ideas? How do you know?
12. Although the king told Haman to carry out his ideas, was Haman happy to do it? Explain
13. True or false, Haman did as the king instructed?
14. This time when Mordecai went to the king's gate, what did Haman do?
15. Was Haman a prejudice racist? Explain
16. Did Haman speak highly of Mordecai to others? Explain

17. What advice was Haman given regarding whether or not to pursue action against Mordecai?
18. What happened next to insure Haman made it to Esther's banquet?

Esther 7

1. What 3 primary guests were at the banquet?
2. Did the king vow again for the third time that he would give Esther anything she wanted?
3. Was there a limit?
4. Did Esther finally reveal what she wanted of the king?
5. What did she request?
6. What was Esther's attitude like when she made the request?
7. Esther said she would not have made a request if the circumstances were different. Explain
8. Was Esther's request urgent? Explain
9. Did the king see Esther's request as urgent? How do you know?
10. How did the king characterize the person responsible for Esther's dilemma?
11. When the king asked who was to blame for Esther's problem, who did she name?
12. How did Esther characterize the person she blamed?
13. When Esther named the perpetrator who caused her problem how did the king react?
14. What was a positive act made in this chapter to control rage?
15. When the problem person was exposed, did this person do anything to make matters better or worse? Explain
16. What did the king's attendants do that signaled the culprit's fate?

17. Name the chamberlain who told the king about the gallows the person built?
18. How high was this gallows?
19. Where was the gallows located?
20. Who do you know that is like this informant?
21. What instigators have you known to watch someone hatch a vicious plot, and say or do nothing to try to talk sense into the person. Yet when the person got found out and was now in trouble the instigators tell all they know against the person?
22. Do you think the informant was thought of as a friend by the perpetrator? Explain
23. Who was planned to be hanged on the gallows?
24. Who ended up being hanged on the gallows?
25. Did this informant say anything that instigated the perpetrator's penalty?
26. What did the informant say that made him look like an evil instigator?
27. Should you be careful of people like this informant who are quick to switch sides and throw others under the bus rather quickly? Do you know anyone who does this?
28. Do you hang around any people who hear you hatching an evil plot and act like they are in support of it, but when it goes bad then tell you how you never should have contemplated such poor decisions?
29. List 5 people that you call your friends, and list the reasons you consider them friends:
30. After the culprit was hanged what happened to the king's anger?
31. Is it important for a leader or authority figure to have control over their anger? Explain

Esther 8

1. What is the significance in who and how Mordecai met king Ahasuerus?
2. When you do not introduce someone you claim to love or respect to your family, what do you think your family is left to conclude about how much you care about the person?
3. What ended up happening to Haman's house?
4. What did the king take back from Haman and give Mordecai?
5. What scripture in Proverbs chapter 13 addresses what happens to the wealth of sinners?
6. When Esther made her request to the king, did it seem unimportant to her? Explain
7. What did she plead with the king to do?
8. How did the king respond?
9. How much did the king trust Esther? Explain
10. Can your parents trust you like king Ahasuerus trusted Esther?
11. What did Haman's letter say was to happen?
12. Are there people like Haman still in positions of authority today?
13. Have you encountered someone who is in a powerful position who has some of the same beliefs as Haman?
14. Is it dangerous to give someone like Haman power? Explain
15. If you were Haman's boss, would you want to be responsible for the things he does when you are not looking?
16. Did you know that parents are less likely to give their children permission and liberties when their youth betray their trust, commit an illegal act, behave irresponsibly or lie to them?

17. Have you done anything that would cause your parents to be hesitant to trust you?
18. When you continue to ask for privileges when you never showed remorse or repentance for prior privileges extended to you that you disregarded and were unappreciative of, why would your parents give you more?
19. Did Esther like to see people hurt and destroyed? Explain
20. Why did king Ahasuerus say Haman was hanged?
21. What did the king give Esther the ability to do?
22. Is this because whatever Esther decided was a decision that would only be in effect 48 hours? Explain
23. How much discretion did the king give Esther?
24. The king also told Esther what to do so her decision would not be amended, what was this?
25. What does this say about how the king felt about Esther?
26. The king had already been betrayed by Haman, and felt disrespected by Queen Vashti, is this good reasons not to ever trust anyone ever again?
27. Which of the four personality types gives people more chances than they deserve and is more likely to allow themselves to be betrayed more than the other 3 personality types?
28. Have you ever had people close to you betray you or let you down? Explain
29. Do you think this gives you good reason not to trust anyone ever again?
30. Who was given permission to dictate a decree to the king's scribes?
31. Who was the decree sent out to and why?
32. Which language(s) was the script(s) sent out in?
33. Is there a reason why they didn't just make a verbal announcement to the people?

34. List all the rules that were followed to attempt to reverse Haman's decree?
35. What unique privilege did the reversal decree grant the Jews?
36. What day was chosen for this event?
37. What needed to happen next?
38. What did the Jews need to be ready that day to do?
39. What did the posts / messengers go out on?
40. Did these posts / messengers take their time doing the king's service?
41. Where was it said the decree was given at?
42. When Mordecai stepped out in royal apparel how did the city react?
43. Find the scripture in Proverbs 29 that makes reference to the type of reaction the people gave Mordecai.
44. Why do you think the Jews were especially happy to see Mordecai in such a high position?
45. Is there anyone you have seen succeed that gave you hope that you could attain what prior to that seemed impossible?
46. What did people who were not Jews decide to do out of fear?
47. Do you know of other circumstances or times when people adopted the traits of another culture to fit in and be relevant with the times?
48. Have you ever felt the need to deny yourself or masquerade as someone other than your authentic self? Explain

Esther 9

1. On what date did the two decrees go into effect?
2. On this date did the enemies of the Jews get what they hoped for? Explain

3. Did the Jews randomly start killing people or go on a killing spree? Explain

4. Were these enemies still comfortable and open about their hatred and contempt for Jews? Explain

5. Were only the citizens in compliance with the decree?

6. What others helped the Jews? Why?

7. What kind of reputation if any did Mordecai have?

8. Was Mordecai soon forgotten about?

9. If Mordecai had tried to take this problem on himself early on and been a violent vigilante do you thing he would have accomplished the same result? Explain

10. What were the Jews permitted to do to their enemies?

11. How many of Haman's sons were affected?

12. What happened to Haman's sons?

13. Did the king ever go to Esther and tell her he made a mistake giving her authority and was putting a stop to the decree she issued? Explain

14. What did the king ask Esther?

15. What was Esther's reply?

16. Was Esther's attitude different now that she had power and her decree had been carried out? Explain

17. If the king granted Esther's request, what was the outcome?

18. What happened to the prey/plunder?

19. The other Jews who gathered were unable to come together and ended up killing each other, true or false?

20. What did people do March 8?

21. What did the Jews at Susa do on the 2nd and 3rd days?

22. Describe the demeanor of the Jews of the villages in unwalled towns:

23. Why do you think Mordecai did what he did in verse 20?

24. What were the people encouraged to do in the future on these two days? Why?

25. Were the Jews receptive to Mordecai's suggestion? What did they do?
26. In your own words, list the events that were recommended the Jews commemorate:
27. What did they call these days?
28. What did the Jews agree to do without fail?
29. How often were they going to celebrate?
30. What days are important to you each year?
31. Do you celebrate them? Why? What significance do they have?
32. Who did they want these important days to be remembered by?
33. What two people wrote another letter?
34. What was this letter supposed to do?
35. Where were the letters sent?
36. What two things did the letter also have words of?
37. What did the letters confirm and/or establish?
38. What happened to Esther's decree?

Esther 10

1. Where were all Mordecai's acts written?
2. Was Mordecai given a lower position or high position? Explain
3. Was Mordecai despised or revered? Explain why

NOTES

Answers

Questions & Answers:

Genesis 2
1. Which day did God bless and sanctify?
   - (3) God blessed the seventh day and sanctified it
2. What did the scripture say God did immediately thereafter?
   - (3) he rested
3. What do you do on the Sabbath?
   - Optional – their honest answer to this question lends its way for great discussions
4. What day of the week is your Sabbath day, if you have one?
   - Optional – their honest answer to this question lends its way for great discussions
5. What weather condition do we experience today that had not happened yet?
   - (5) no rain yet
6. What was formed from dust?
   - (7) man was formed from the dust of the ground
7. What happened that caused what was formed to breathe and come to life?

- (7) the Lord God breathed into his nostrils the breath of life and man became living
8. Who made every tree?
   - (9) the Lord God made every tree
9. How were the trees described?
   - (9) pleasant to the sight to grow, and good for food
10. What were the two distinctions between trees?
    - (9) the tree of life and the tree of knowledge of good and evil
11. What is the name of the second river?
    - (13) And the name of the second river is Gihon
12. What land does this river surround/encompass?
    - (13) it compasseth the whole land of Ethiopia
13. What reason did God put man in the garden?
    - (15) God put the man into the garden of Eden to dress it and keep it
14. What is another way of describing the reason God put man in the garden?
    - Optional – their honest answer to this question lends its way for great discussions
    - He told man what his purpose was
    - He gave him a job
    - He blessed him with a place to be and then gave him responsibility to care for his blessing
15. What freedom did God give Adam concerning the trees?
    - (16) Here's the rule – you can eat freely of every tree of the garden (freedom & liberty was given)
16. What one boundary or restriction did God give Adam concerning the trees?
    - (17) Except the tree of the knowledge of good and evil don't eat
17. What was he told would happen if the man broke this rule?

- (17) "The day you eat of it you will die"
18. Is it important to have boundaries? Explain
    - Optional – their honest answer to this question lends its way for great discussions
    - Yes.
    - They provide order, morality and safety. Without them everyone would just do what feels good to them and infringe upon the rights of others.
    - Our flesh often disagrees with our spiritual compass and rules and boundaries help direct us in the right way.
19. List at least 3 freedoms or blessings your parents have given you:
    - Optional – their honest answer to this question lends its way for great discussions
    - I have my own room
    - I drive a car
    - I get to stay home alone when they are gone
    - I have a cell phone they pay for
    - I have internet access
    - I have choices of what I want to eat at home from groceries my parents purchase
20. List at least 3 boundaries your parents have for you:
    - Optional – their honest answer to this question lends its way for great discussions
    - Keep your room clean and maintained
    - Get insurance and drive safely
    - Do not let anyone into the home while parents are gone
    - Obey the law
    - Go to school and be respectful and come straight home afterwards
    - Do not access restricted websites and material online

- Eat healthy foods and well balanced meals
21. What was it God said was not good about man's circumstances?
    - (18) God said, it is not good that man was alone
22. What did God decide was the solution?
    - (18) I will make him a help meet
23. What was the problem God had with naming the creatures?
    - (19) & (20) God did not name them, Adam named every living creature
24. What did God cause to happen to Adam?
    - (21) the Lord God caused a deep sleep to fall upon Adam
25. Briefly describe the first reported surgery and who performed it:
    - (21) God took one of Adam's ribs and closed up his flesh
26. What did God make during this procedure?
    - (22) Of this rib the Lord God made a woman
27. How was this gift God made Adam introduced?
    - (22) God brought (presented) her to Adam.
28. What did Adam say that let us know he recognized she was a part of him?
    - (23) "This is now bone of my bones, and flesh of my flesh...because she was taken out of Man"
29. Who named her and what was she named?
    - (23) Adam named her Woman
30. What is the reason a man should leave his father and mother?
    - (24) to cleave unto his wife to become one flesh
31. What condition were they in that may cause others to be embarrassed or ashamed?

- (25) They were both naked and not ashamed (innocence)
32. Describe a situation where you were not ashamed until someone said something to you?
    - Optional – their honest answer to this question lends its way for great discussions
    - Hug and kiss parents in public
    - Pray over your food
    - Tell the truth
    - Volunteer and admit to wrongdoing
    - Return money or property

Genesis 3

1. What was the shrewdest and most subtle beast of the field?
    - (1) The serpent
2. How was this beast made?
    - (1) We only know that God made it
3. What unique abilities did this beast have that it no longer has?
    - The ability to speak
    - The ability to communicate and reason with humans
4. What was the first thing this beast challenged?
    - (1) He challenged their knowledge of the rules, and what God told them
        - (1) "Didn't God say you could eat from every tree in the garden?"
5. Who do you allow to speak to you and influence your decisions?
    - Optional – their honest answer to this question lends its way for great discussions
6. Why was the serpent making this his business? Why was he asking about what *they* could do and eat?

- Optional – their honest answer to this question lends its way for great discussions
- He wanted to see if he could trick them.
- He wanted to get them into trouble.
- He was probably curious to see what the repercussions were if he got them to eat the fruit.

7. Have you ever had others question you about the rules your parents gave you? Explain
   - Optional – their honest answer to this question lends its way for great discussions

8. What are some counterpunches you could use in the future?
   - Optional – their honest answer to this question lends its way for great discussions
   - Why are you asking?
   - Worry about yourself and not what my parents told me.
   - I am not inviting you or your opinion into what I was told to do, it doesn't concern you

9. Do you think others are asking questions to help you obey?
   - Optional – their honest answer to this question lends its way for great discussions
   - NO!

10. What are some good solutions to avoid being tricked and manipulated by others to break the rules?
    - Know the rules
    - Follow the rules
    - Don't engage with those trying to get you to sin
    - Put a stop to conversations that try to lead you astray

11. What were the biggest mistakes these two made?
    - Optional – their honest answer to this question lends its way for great discussions
    - Listening to the serpent.

- Not realizing if the serpent really wanted to know what God said, he would have asked God?
- (2) She answered the serpent and explained to him her understanding, "We may eat of the fruit of the trees of the garden, yes."
- The serpent started out with something they could agree with so they would let their guard down. It seemed like a harmless discussion, but it clearly was not, and they shouldn't have spoken with him.

12. What did she say God's boundary was regarding what they could eat?
- (3) "But not the fruit of the tree in the center of the garden." God said, "Ye shall not eat of it, neither shall ye touch it, lest ye die."

13. Did the woman relay God's rule correctly or add or delete instructions? Explain
- She was incorrect because she added information
- God said nothing about touching it

14. What rules have you misinterpreted or altered in the past so you could do what you wanted?
- Optional – their honest answer to this question lends its way for great discussions
- Not come straight home from school
- Telling yourself if you don't get caught then what you did was not wrong

15. What laws or rules in society do you see being modified and misconstrued so people can sin? Explain
- Optional – their honest answer to this question lends its way for great discussions
- People who are not married were forbidden from living together (cohabitating) as if they were
- Alcohol was illegal and was later legalized

- Marijuana has become legalized
- Abortions have become legal
- People are open now and less ashamed about fornicating

16. Would it have been easier to have the rule in writing to refer to?
    - Optional – their honest answer to this question lends its way for great discussions

17. Still today people are more trusting with their friends and family. They choose to make verbal arrangements and not put their agreement in writing. Is this wise? Explain
    - Optional – their honest answer to this question lends its way for great discussions
    - No.
    - God is perfect and He makes His commands clear. He put His commandments and rules in writing for our benefit. Humans are imperfect and it is best to have our agreements in writing so that the terms are clear and able to be referred back to later.

18. What does the serpent's behavior tell you about outsiders who have an opinion or curiosity about rules your parents have given you for your own good?
    - To be leery of anyone asking you about the rules given to you to follow
    - Avoid people trying to tell you how to get around those rules
    - It may not be a good idea to listen to people telling you what to do who don't have to bear the consequences
    - If you have questions or concerns about your parent's rules, clear it up with your parents.

19. Do you think having the rules in writing prevents people from doing the wrong thing?

- Optional – their honest answer to this question lends its way for great discussions
- No. People who are determined to do wrong, will do wrong. It only takes away most of their excuses when they had a copy of the rules in writing but chose to disregard them.

20. What purpose is there for having rules or agreements in writing? Does it make a difference? Explain
    - Optional – their honest answer to this question lends its way for great discussions
    - It documents and brings clarity as to what the rules are
    - Yes, it can make a difference
    - It can eliminate or minimize arguments about any fact or term that was clearly agreed to in writing

21. The serpent said, "You won't die." Why should this have been the biggest red flag to stop talking and listening to the serpent?
    - Anytime anyone tells you to go against what God has said to do or not do you should not listen to or associate with them

22. The serpent said, "Because God knows if you eat you'll be like him, your mind will be opened and you'll know good from evil." Some of what the serpent said was true but it was twisted truth. Explain
    - Optional – their honest answer to this question lends its way for great discussions
    - It is true they would be like God after eating the fruit. They were already like God. That's like telling you if your last name is Jones, that if you drink alcohol your last name will be Jones.
    - It is true their disobedience opened their eyes to evil, before that they only knew about good. Once they

sinned they quickly learned to be ashamed, separate, blame, lost their innocence and learned to hide.

23. Do you know of other promotions or commercials, that only give partial or misleading endorsements promoting heavenly results without telling you the true cost and side effects? Give some examples:

- Optional – their honest answer to this question lends its way for great discussions

- Exposing your body to premature risk and danger to attempt to rid yourself of uncomfortable feelings, pain and preconceived inadequacies (sex changes, prescription medication, cosmetic surgeries, diet pills, Botox injections, butt implants, unlicensed procedures, abortions, premarital sex/fornication, contraceptives, bulimia, anorexia, cutting, mutilation, etc.)

- Abortions – the lies are, "It's just a blob of flesh, it's not a baby. You can't be kept back with this baby you have your whole life ahead of you. What about you? You have your needs. Who are they to tell you what to do? Get rid of it. You have rights. Just do it! Quickly. Don't think about it again. The law says you can make the choice for yourself. Can't you decide for yourself? Don't tell the father, he'll tell you what to do. It's your body, your baby, your choice alone! Don't tell your parents.

- Advertisements would lead people to believe condoms, birth control, limiting your partners, having feelings for your partner, moving in – *shacking up*, and simply professing your love is safe sex.
    - o Making a verbal promise without a written commitment recognized by law or by God is not safe sex

- o Safe sex is no premarital sex, it is monogamy and commitment to be loyal to your spouse.
- You've never lived with a mate before, you need the experience
  - o No! Do not play house it is fornication. Get married then live with your spouse.
- How do you know if you are sexually compatible unless you have sex first?
  - o Marriage comes before sex

24. What lies and negative self-talk comes to your mind that make you question your parent's rules?
- Optional – their honest answer to this question lends its way for great discussions
- They are holding out on you and do not want you to know the truth
- They lied to you
- Parents say that because they do not want you to have fun and enjoy yourself
- Parents are out of touch and just do not understand that times have changed

25. What is a good counterpunch to use when someone is telling you God's rules will ruin your fun?
- Optional – their honest answer to this question lends its way for great discussions
- No good thing will He withhold from us if we walk uprightly (*Psalm 84:11*)
- If there's something we are being sheltered from now, I trust Him (God), it's for my own good

26. We have decided as a society youth do not have the brain development and authority to make certain decisions until 18 years of age. Is this meant to protect youth or hurt youth? Explain

- It's for their protection
- It gives them time to develop, mature and grow into a responsible adult

27. It is hard to retain knowledge, understanding and rules that is why it is important for adults to find ways of reminding you constantly in order for you to automatically react properly. Without practice and repetition, you are prone to forget the rules and boundaries God and society have set. What examples can you list of things or routines that are taught to indoctrinate youth of beliefs and rules?
    - Prayer before service, eating, bedtime, and before leaving the home
    - Saying the pledge of allegiance at government meetings and at school
    - Eating 3 balanced meals a day
    - Brushing your teeth
    - Bathing
    - Putting clothes on before going out in public
    - Attending church
    - Household chores
    - Saying "please" and "thank you"

28. Have there been any rulers, leaders, or presidents who have used the youth as a tool to divide the family? Explain
    - Optional – their honest answer to this question lends its way for great discussions
    - Hitler. He introduced a divide between youth and parents, and encouraged youth to report parents. His goal was to take the authority from the parents and have control relinquished to the government.

29. Before we sin or are disobedient, often one or more of our 5 senses engages our mind to create a convincing self-dialogue for us to act. What are the 5 senses?

- Sight – Smell – Touch – Taste - Hearing
30. Can you see why food is such a huge temptation in the Bible and in life? Explain how it engages our senses:
    - Sight – it looks appetizing and delicious
    - Smell – the aromas get our attention
    - Touch – the melt in your mouth, crunch, juicy delight of the appropriate texture of foods is quite appealing
    - Taste – the sweet, spicy, flavorful bites of comfort foods awaken the taste buds
    - Hearing – the sound of bubbling, sizzling, crackling foods cooking or baking are familiar attractions
31. What excuses do you think were being played in their heads to prompt Adam and Eve to sin?
    - Optional – their honest answer to this question lends its way for great discussions
    - You can trust the woman, take it
    - What the serpent said makes sense
    - The fruit does look delicious. It seems a waste not to eat it
    - The woman ate it and nothing happened to her, it must be okay
    - It looks like God is holding out on us and withholding this good fruit from us to keep us from becoming more like Him
    - I wonder why He told us not to eat this fruit? It looks perfectly edible
32. Which of the five senses got the woman's attention? Explain
    - (6) Vision.
    - (6) And when the woman *saw* the tree was good for food
    - (6) It was *pleasant to the eyes*

33. Why did she desire the tree, what did she think it could do for her?
    - Optional – their honest answer to this question lends its way for great discussions
    - (6) make her wise
34. What did she do next and who did she involve?
    - (6) she took of the fruit, ate, gave to her husband with her and he ate
35. What do you think came to mind when each one was called out on their own sin?
    - Optional – their honest answer to this question lends its way for great discussions
    - If Adam had done what he was supposed to and dealt with the serpent himself, this wouldn't have happened
    - If God never would have given me the woman, this wouldn't have happened
    - If the woman hadn't spoken to the serpent and listened to him, this never would have happened
    - It's all Adam's fault, he's the one God directly told what the rule was
    - It's not my fault Adam and Eve were so gullible, I'm not the one who disobeyed, they did
36. What did sin and disobedience do to this couple and forever change?
    - Optional – their honest answer to this question lends its way for great discussions
    - (7) both their eyes were open and they knew they were naked. Their innocence was lost.
        - They discovered something that wasn't necessary or important to know at that time
    - (7) they sewed fig leaves together and made themselves aprons

- o They increased their work load and efforts to now cover themselves and hide
- They were tricked into surrendering their privileges and freedom
    - o They let someone less knowledgeable than God convince them it was okay to act outside of the boundaries He set. They lost the privilege of being in such a perfect place, and showed they were not ready to handle the freedoms afforded them
- (10) Just as evidenced by Adam trying to hide from the presence of God, sin separates us from God and those we love and care about and who love and care about us.
    - o *But your iniquities have separated between you and your God, and your sins have hid his face from you, that he will not hear.   Isaiah 59:2*
- They were now body conscious and ashamed
- They broke trust. They lost faith in what God told them and let the serpent put doubt in their minds. They believed what the serpent said over what God told them.

37. Sin can prematurely open your eyes to evil and upset your spirit and your conscience. Name some temptations people fall for listening to the media, peers, and others. Also, list some of the consequences that result that you don't find out about unless you fall prey to the temptation or sin?
    - Premarital sex – lose innocence, feel guilt, contract STD's, teen pregnancy, and self-image is damaged
    - Drugs – lose will, addiction, overdose, health problems, fear, arrests, and lie

- Abortion – guilt, shame, innocence lost, deciding to end the life of an innocent baby/your child, cover up, regret, lies
- Cheating – lose trust, lose respect, lack control, destroy relationships, keep secrets, sneak, dishonesty and hide
- Junk Food – damage self-control, satisfy craving and surrender will, obesity, diabetes, health issues
- Refuse to work & don't do chores – being idle, vulnerable to suggestions & sin, easily led astray, lazy, entitled, rebellion & inactivity can result in health issues

38. What are some counterpunches you could use in the future if someone is trying to persuade you to disregard your parent's instructions and God's laws?
    - Optional – their honest answer to this question lends its way for great discussions
    - "Stay on course"
    - "Don't stray from doing the right thing"
    - "Guard your heart"
    - "Don't listen to them, do what your parents told you to"
    - "I will be selective who gets to speak in my ears"
    - "What they are saying goes against the Bible and my parent's rules, I'm blocking them"
    - "What they are telling me to do does not line up with scripture, my purpose, and what God told me. I'm walking away from them and shutting them out"

39. It is said that sin causes a divide and separation from God. Is this demonstrated in this chapter? After Adam and the woman sinned, describe their next interaction with God:
    - (8) They heard the voice of God walking in the garden in the cool of the day, Adam and his wife hid themselves from the presence of the Lord God amongst the trees of the garden

40. Do you know how Adam and Eve felt? Have you ever sinned against God and decided to avoid the church, your parents or other Christians? Explain
    - Optional – their honest answer to this question lends its way for great discussions
41. Have you ever been involved in doing something your parents have told you not to do, and been startled by their voice calling you or them calling your phone? Have you found yourself avoiding them, hiding, or having a strained conversation to hide what you have done or were about to do? Explain
    - Optional – their honest answer to this question lends its way for great discussions
42. What did God ask Adam?
    - (9) The Lord God called Adam, "Where are you?"
43. What do you think the significance was in God asking Adam this question, we know God knew the answer to?
    - Optional – their honest answer to this question lends its way for great discussions
    - To give Adam an opportunity to admit what he did wrong and repent
    - To cause Adam to examine himself and where he was and what he had done
    - He wanted Adam to take a look at where he was and what he chose to run from trying to conceal his sin
    - To cause Adam to look at himself, see that he was not in his rightful place and purpose
    - To make Adam realize he was no longer reflecting God's image and likeness but had taken on the serpent's image that was one of secrets, deception, blaming, avoidance, shame, and confusion

- He was giving Adam an opportunity to correct and rectify his situation and circumstances

44. What was Adam's answer to the question God asked?
   - (10) He said, "I heard your voice and I was afraid, because I was naked and I hid myself.

45. Why do you think Adam's response hurt him rather than help him?
   - First he was asked a simple question he didn't answer but proceeded to run his mouth with excuses

46. What did Adam's answer to God reveal?
   - That Adam had allowed someone else to influence his decisions
   - That he was experiencing negative reactions that would not have come about if Adam had not listened to adverse influences

47. What were the next two questions God asked Adam?
   - (11) And he said, "Who told thee that thou wast naked?"
   - (11) "Hast thou eaten of the tree, whereof I commanded thee that thou shouldest not eat?"

48. When you disobey your parents and let someone evil speak in your ear to you, what is bound to occur?
   - Sin
   - Confusion
   - Consequences & punishment
   - Trust issues
   - You lose liberties and freedoms
   - It changes you

49. Did Adam take responsibility for what he did? If he didn't own up to his part, who did Adam blame?
   - (12) No

- (12) This woman that you gave me, she gave me of the tree and I did eat.
- (12) The man was first and quickest to blame the woman and God.

50. What did the Lord ask the woman?
- (13) The Lord asked the woman, "What is this that thou hast done?"

51. What did the woman answer?
- (13) The woman said, "The serpent beguiled me, and I did eat."

52. Did the woman accept responsibility for what she did or blame others?
- (13) She blamed the serpent
- She too did not answer the question of what *she* did, but began to point the finger at the serpent

53. Who is responsible for what you do?
- You are

54. Is it an excuse if someone tells you to do something your parents have told you not to do? Explain
- No
- You are accountable for what your parents told you to do. You are responsible for what you do

55. Did God reprimand anyone else other than Adam and the woman? Explain
- (14) Yes
- (14) The Lord God told the serpent, "because thou has done this thou art cursed above all cattle, and above every beast in the field

56. What was the serpent's curse/punishment?
- (14) upon thy belly shalt thou go, and dust shalt thou eat all the days of thy life

57. Based on the serpent's punishment/curse, what may that mean as to how he was formed prior?
- Optional – their honest answer to this question lends its way for great discussions
- He possibly stood upright like a human does

58. What else is different about the serpent then and now?
- The serpent had logic and the same language to be able to communicate with us but no more since we listened to it

59. What else can we learn from the interaction between the serpent, Adam and the woman?
- Optional – their honest answer to this question lends its way for great discussions
- Adam and the woman had dominion over all the animals (Genesis 1:26) but let something they had dominion over entice them to sin.

60. Before you judge Adam and the woman, ask yourself, "What am I currently allowing to tell me what to do, that I have dominion over?
- Optional – their honest answer to this question lends its way for great discussions
- My body, lust, porn, drugs, cigarettes, vaping, girls/boys, alcohol, anger, fighting, temper, enemies, food, sugar, laziness, phone, internet, texting, hate, unforgiveness, Playstation, TV, radio, music, dance, sex, social media, someone younger

61. Is the woman's seed/offspring and the serpent's seed/offspring enemies?
- (15) Yes. God said, we will bruise its head and they would bruise our heel.

62. What was the woman's curse?

- (16) Unto the woman God said I will greatly multiply thy sorrow and thy conception; in sorrow thou shalt bring forth children; and thy desire shall be for thy husband and he shall rule over thee.

63. The woman's punishment was to have great sorrow during what times?
    - Conception and childbirth
64. What did God say Adam did wrong?
    - (17) unto Adam God said, because you listened to your wife, ate of the tree which I commanded you, "Thou shalt not eat of it"
65. What consequences resulted from Adam's mistakes?
    - (17) The ground is cursed.
    - (17) In sorrow you shall eat of it all the days of your life.
    - (18) Thorns also and thistles shall it bring forth to thee
66. What did God curse?
    - (17) The ground is cursed.
67. What must he do all the days of his life?
    - (17) In sorrow you shall eat of it all the days of your life.
68. What were they destined to eat?
    - (18) and thou shalt eat the herb of the fields;
69. What were they now required to do the remainder of their lives to eat
    - (19) sweat/labor
70. What was Adam told he was made of and would eventually return to?
    - (19) Dust of the ground
71. What did Adam rename the woman?
    - (20) Adam called his wife, Eve
72. What did her name mean?
    - (20) she was the mother of all living.
73. What was made for Adam and his wife to clothe them?

- (21) coats of skins

74. Who made it?
    - (21) God made coats of skins and clothed Adam and his wife
75. The Lord God proclaimed that Adam now had what newfound knowledge?
    - (22) Adam knew good and evil
76. How long would man live if he ate from the tree of life?
    - (22) If he also takes of the tree of life and eats he will live forever.
77. What were they banished from the garden of Eden to do?
    - (23) to cultivate/work the ground from which he was made from
78. What beings were placed east of Eden?
    - (24) Cherubims/mighty angelic beings
79. What object was turned every way to keep and guard the way of the tree of life?
    - (24) A flaming sword

Extra Credit Questions:

80. What did Adam and the woman eat that Adam was told not to eat? What scripture(s) support and confirm your answer?
- Fruit of the tree of the knowledge of good and evil
- But <u>of the tree of the knowledge of good and evil</u>, thou shalt not eat of it: for in the day that thou eatest thereof thou shalt surely die.   Genesis 2:17 KJV
- And when the woman saw that the tree was good for food, and that it was pleasant to the eyes, and a tree to be desired to make one wise, she <u>took of the fruit</u> thereof, <u>and did eat</u>, and gave also unto her husband with her; and he did eat. Genesis 3:6 KJV

81. If I were to ask most ministers and most people, the prior question (#80) what answer would they give me?
- An apple – there is no scripture reference that supports this
82. Why is it important to get our answers and wisdom from scriptures?
- Optional – their honest answer to this question lends its way for great discussions
- Because the scriptures have the truth in writing for us to read ourselves
- People often interpret what they read or relay what they heard
- Right and wrong is too important to allow another person to translate and decipher for you. Always pray and study The Bible for yourself to confirm, clarify or repudiate your understanding

NOTES

The Temptation of Jesus – Matthew 4:1-11

Questions & Answers

1. Who or what led Jesus into the wilderness?
   a. (1) The Spirit
2. Who or what was going to tempt Jesus?
   a. (1) The devil
3. What did Jesus do that caused him to be hungry?
   a. (2) he fasted
4. How long did he do this?
   a. (2) 40 days and forty nights
5. What was the very first 7 words the tempter said to Jesus?
   a. (3) "If thou be the son of God"
6. Why is this important?
   a. Optional – their honest answer to this question lends its way for great discussions
   b. He was challenging Jesus' identity to see if he could get Him to act beneath his calling & status
   c. Any person who doesn't know his purpose or who he is can be easily manipulated
7. Have you ever gotten angry because someone called you out of your name?

    a. Optional – their honest answer to this question lends its way for great discussions
8. What difference does it make if others fail to know or acknowledge who you are, as long as the people who matter know you?
    a. Optional – their honest answer to this question lends its way for great discussions
9. What did the tempter tell Jesus to do to prove who Jesus was?
    a. (3) "command that these stones be made bread"
10. Have you ever been told to do something or challenged to prove something to others?
    a. Optional – their honest answer to this question lends its way for great discussions
    b. Accused of being "weak" or a "coward" if you don't fight
    c. Told you are not Christian if you refuse to give others what they want / their way
11. What was Jesus' response?
    a. (40) "It is written, Man shall not live by bread alone, but by every word that proceedeth out of the mouth of God"
12. What did Jesus' response mean?
    a. Food is not the only thing that gives a man life each day. The word of God is necessary to feed our spirit daily.
13. Where was Jesus taken next?
    a. (5) Up into the holy city
14. Who took him there?
    a. (5) The devil
15. Where was Jesus put?
    a. (5) On a pinnacle of the temple
16. This time what was the first 7 words said to Jesus?
    a. (6) "If thou be the son of God"
17. What was Jesus told to do to prove himself this time?

    a. (6) "Cast thyself down"
18. What 3 words did the devil use to support his position?
    a. (6) "It is written"
19. Why are these three words so important?
    a. Optional – their honest answer to this question lends its way for great discussions
    b. The devil knew Jesus was someone who followed the scriptures
    c. It was a test to see how knowledgeable Jesus was of the scriptures
20. What protection was Jesus told he had?
    a. (6) "He shall give his angels charge concerning thee: and in their hands they shall bear thee up, lest at any time thou dash thy foot against a stone."
21. List some examples of assurances instigators give people that are unreliable:
    a. Optional – their honest answer to this question lends its way for great discussions
    b. You won't get caught
    c. We'll back you up, don't worry
    d. Just say you were with me and I'll be your alibi
22. What initial words did Jesus say in response?
    a. (7) "It is written"
23. What did Jesus say about temptation?
    a. (7) "Thou shalt not tempt the Lord thy God"
24. What did Jesus mean by this?
    a. Optional – their honest answer to this question lends its way for great discussions
    b. Just because God can save your life doesn't mean you should kill yourself on a dare to then ask God to bring you back to life to prove something to someone else
25. Where was Jesus taken next, and by who?

    a. (8) into an exceeding high mountain
    b. (8) the devil
26. What was he shown?
    a. (8) All the kingdoms of the world, and the glory of them
27. Jesus was offered these things if Jesus agreed to do what?
    a. (9) If Jesus would fall down and worship the devil
28. What did Jesus say in response?
    a. (10) "Get thee hence, Satan: for it is written, Thou shalt worship the Lord thy God, and him only shalt thou serve"
29. What did the devil do next?
    a. The devil left him
30. What positive thing occurred in the end?
    a. (11) Angels came and ministered unto Jesus
31. What does this passage of scripture demonstrate to you?
    a. Optional – their honest answer to this question lends its way for great discussions
    b. You too may expect to be challenged repeatedly on your identity, faith, and knowledge of the scriptures
    c. If you persevere and respond with God's word, the devil will leave you alone and get shut down
32. If Jesus had become violent or enraged at having one challenge back to back, do you think he would have had the same outcome? Explain
    a. Optional – their honest answer to this question lends its way for great discussions
    b. No. A person who escalates a debate into violence is someone out of control
    c. No. Jesus stayed calm, and unashamedly corrected the devil on the devil's scripture quotes. The devil had no retort and ultimately gave up and left

NOTES

Bad News – Matthew 4:12-17

Questions & Answers:

1. What happened before this next reading assignment?
- After Satan tried to tempt Jesus and Jesus was victorious, the devil left him
2. Jesus receives news, what was he told?
- (12) John was cast into prison (arrested)
3. He left what place to go where?
- (12) he left Judea and returned to Galilee
4. Did he go to see John, protest, or get him out of prison? Explain
- (13) No. He left Nazareth and dwelt in Capernaum
5. What untrue criticisms do you think friends, family and others would later say about Jesus for doing this?
- Jesus was not compassionate
- He had a massive ego and was more dedicated to starting his own ministry than to be supportive of his family
- He should have had his first miracle and freed John from prison
- He cared more about his own image than supporting his

cousin who was a passionate advocate
- He was jealous of John
- He was weak and afraid to fight on John's behalf
6. Do you think anyone understood at the time why Jesus did not immediately go to John's defense? Explain
- Optional – their honest answer to this question lends its way for great discussions
- No one but God
- I believe only God understood because Jesus was submitted to God and got his marching orders only from Him
7. What can Christ's response teach you?
- Don't be quick to act on my own emotions
- When I am about to be taken to the next level of ministry, my call or my purpose in life, expect bad news
- I can anticipate trouble and situations to come about and attempt to take me off course
- There will always be critics with opinions about everything I say and do, I am to not let it take me off the right path
8. Have you ever been in a situation where what you knew was the right thing to do was guaranteed to attract criticism from strangers and those close to you? Explain
- Optional – their honest answer to this question lends its way for great discussions
9. Knowing what we know now, if you had an opportunity to encourage Jesus at this beginning stage, what would you have said to him?
- Optional – their honest answer to this question lends its way for great discussions
- Do not be discouraged
- You will get through this with flying colors, be encouraged
- This is part of the process, you are on the right track

- Do not let the opinions of people influence your decisions
- Keep following God's direction for your life and you will succeed and never fail
- John is doing what he is supposed to do and you must do what you are supposed to do and not divert from that
10. Was Jesus conscious of living a life on purpose and not acting on his own? Explain
- Yes
- (14) The reason he traveled the course he did was to fulfill scripture
- (14) Esaias the prophet spoke a prophesy that needed to be fulfilled and would not have been had he done his own thing
11. What was the prophesy spoken and who spoke it?
- (16) The people which sat in darkness saw great light; and to them which sat in the region and shadow of death light is sprung up
- (14) Esaias
12. Because of his obedience, what began to happen for Jesus next?
- (17) Jesus began to preach
13. What was his first recorded message centered around?
- (17) repentance
- (17) He said, "Repent: for the kingdom of heaven is at hand"
14. What does Christ's message mean to you?
- Optional – their honest answer to this question lends its way for great discussions
- Surrender your life to the Lord God, turn from your worldly ways. The Lord is here in the flesh to show us that heaven is within reach of anyone willing to accept the invitation

Extra credit questions:

15. What scriptures in The Bible address the timing of the enemy's attacks on our lives?
- Optional – their honest answer to this question lends its way for great discussions
- Matthew 13:19 KJV
    - When any one heareth the word of the kingdom, and understandeth it not, then cometh the wicked one, and catcheth away that which was sown in his heart. This is he which receiveth seed by the way side.
- Mark 4:15 KJV
    - And these are they by the way side, where the word is sown; but when they have heard, Satan cometh immediately, and taketh away the word that was sown in their hearts.

16. Every stage of life is important and a part of life. List the scriptures that tell us trials and temptations are not strange _(A)_ nor uncommon _(B)_. We can rest in knowing that we can endure troubles because of the joy of the anticipated end result _(C)_.
- Optional – their honest answer to this question lends its way for great discussions
- (A) 1 Peter 4:12 KJV
    - (12) Beloved, think it not strange concerning the fiery trial which is to try you, as though some strange thing happened unto you:
- (B) 1 Corinthians 10:13 KJV
    - There hath no temptation taken you but such as is common to man: but God is faithful, who will not

> suffer you to be tempted above that ye are able; but will with the temptation also make a way of escape, that ye may be able to bear it.

- (C) Hebrews 12:2 KJV
  - Looking unto Jesus the author and finisher of our faith; who for the joy that was set before him endured the cross, despising the shame, and is set down at the right hand of the throne of God.

17. This lesson is a reminder of what?
- Optional – their honest answer to this question lends its way for great discussions
- Wisdom and knowledge of the scriptures is key to righteous living
- We can expect with each enlightenment to be challenged by the enemy to see if we truly believe what we learned
- There are going to be several opportunities in life that will attempt to take us off course and try to divert us from our purpose and calling in life. It is up to us to prioritize our lives and stay on track
- Only what we do for Christ will last

NOTES

Esther – Chapters 1-10

Questions & Answers

Esther 1
1. What was the limit the king placed on wine consumption?
*   (7-8) None
*   (7KJV/7NLT) – drinks were served in abundance just as the king commanded/according to the state of the king
*   (8KJV/8NLT) – the only requirement/law on drinking was not to compel anyone to consume any more than they wanted, each person could decide for themselves what amount that was and set their own limit
2. What was the first law, rule or stipulation mentioned in Esther 1?
*   (8KJV/8NLT) – the only requirement/law on drinking was not to compel anyone to consume any more than they wanted, each person could decide for themselves what amount that was and set their own limit
3. Is it a good idea for people to decide to consume as much alcohol as they want? Explain
*   No. People would get drunk and act irrational in public. There needs to be boundaries

4. If you were having a party at your home would you have this same rule? What if you had a job as a judge or well-known political leader that came with a lot of responsibility and public/civic recognition?

- No, I wouldn't serve alcohol in my home. I wouldn't want the liability and responsibility
- I'd have to be even more careful if I had a high ranking job

5. The king was intoxicated, is this appropriate behavior for a king?

- No. Leaders are to be sober and not corrupt justice or the law

6. What scriptures in The Bible address intoxication and whether a king or leader should drink or be intoxicated?

- Proverbs 31:4
- Proverbs 31:5
- Ephesians 5:18
- Christians need sober thinking and virtuous influences in serving the spiritual interests of people

7. Why was the king calling for Queen Vashti?

- (10-12) – the king was intoxicated and he commanded his staff to show off / parade his wife Vashti.

8. Did his staff do the right thing in carrying out the king's request, or should they have tried to talk him out of it?

- His advisers and close confidants should have tried to talk him out of it and talk sense into him.

9. Did Queen Vashti do the right thing, or should she have handled it differently?

- She could have given him more respect and not dismissed the king in front of others.

10. If you were Queen Vashti, what would you have done?

- Tried to operate within the law and handle it respectfully.

11. Is this the kind of behavior of a male who cares about a female, or is this the behavior of a drunk male showing off?
- It was the behavior of a drunk male showing off
- It was the juvenile act of an inebriated man who wasn't regarding his queen with love and respect. He was treating her like property to put on display.
12. What was the king's response?
- (11) the king was "very wroth" (angry)
13. Did the king have a right to be angry? Explain
- Optional – their honest answer to this question lends its way for great discussions
14. Do you think this would have happened if the king had been sober? Explain
- Probably not. One who is intoxicated will often do things they would never do if they were sober.
15. Do people normally make better decisions the more alcohol they consume or the soberer they are?
- Generally, and typically the soberer they are they make better decisions
16. Were there any anger symptoms listed that should have given the king warning to reverse the symptoms?
- (11) his anger "burned in him."
17. Did the king immediately react pleased with Queen Vashti?
- (11) No. He was very wroth
18. Should the king have immediately responded?
- No. He should have sobered up first.
19. Does this king sound like a bad or violent man? Explain
- Optional – their honest answer to this question lends its way for great discussions
- No. No violent tendencies were apparent
20. Why do you think he consulted advisers and not strangers, friends or relatives?

- Optional – their honest answer to this question lends its way for great discussions
- He wanted to do the right thing and operate within the law
- Friends & relatives may have sided with him & enabled him
21. What was the king's intent for contacting advisers?
- Although angry and intoxicated, to respond within legal guidelines of a king
22. What was the expertise of the advisers the king consulted?
- (13) – the king consulted his advisers immediately who knew the law and judgments / Persian laws & customs
23. Was Memucan's advice given in the best interest of the people or self-serving? What should this teach you to be cautious of?
- Self-serving and chauvinistic.
- Beware of instigators who want you to set an example or do something they refuse to do
24. What dangerous distorted thinking and anger pattern were being promoted in verse 18?
- distorted thinking (mind reading)
- anger pattern (anticipatory anger)
25. Does putting a rule in writing and making it into law change a person's rebellious heart?
- No. There are no guarantees
26. Was this thought out enough and with the right people deciding whether it should become a law or not?
- No. It appeared these men were manipulating the king and taking advantage of his drunken state to get control of their wives
27. Do you think the king took Memucan's suggestion because he was offended or because he thought it would help strengthen couples' relationships?
- Because he was offended

28. What did the king do to make sure everyone was made aware of this new law?
- Put it in writing
- Notified all provinces
- Put it in every language
29. The rule to let guests be carefree and drink as much as they want are characteristics of what personality type?
- Funnies
30. When king Ahasuerus went to his advisers and wanted to punish Vashti within their law, this is a characteristic of what personality type?
- Bookie

Esther 2:
1. Verse 1 says the king cooled off and remembered what Vashti did and what he decreed against her. What does this tell us about his rationale before?
- That he was drunk and angry before
- He wasn't thinking clearly when he made such an important decision
- He was in no condition to be making a permanent law
- He acted and made a law to punish and retaliate against Vashti but it would affect all the women
- He had regret and remorse/guilt
2. Why were virgins preferred to be the king's wife?
- Being a virgin is a strong positive character trait
- It exemplifies a woman of good morals
3. Did the king like Esther?
- (9) Yes
4. Was she liked any more than other women by the king? How do you know?

- (9) Yes. Verse 9 said the king selected and preferred Esther
5. What advice did Mordecai give Esther? Why?
- (10) & (20) to conceal her nationality (Jewish) and family background
6. If you were given this same advice would it upset you? Explain
- Optional and variety of answers acceptable as long as they are honest
7. Have you ever been told this before, to deny a part of who you are? If you answered yes, how did it make you feel?
- Optional and variety of answers acceptable as long as they are honest
8. Why do you think Mordecai told Esther to keep this information about herself private?
- Optional – their honest answer to this question lends its way for great discussions
- He knew there were people who hated Jews who may use this information to hurt Esther
9. What plot did Mordecai find out about? What if anything did he do about it?
- (21-23) Mordecai was working at the palace and found out two of the king's eunuch's (Bigthan & Teresh) were angry with the king and plotted to assassinate him. Mordecai told Esther
10. Did anyone else do anything about this information Mordecai had?
- Esther told the king. An investigation confirmed the plot and Bigthan and Teresh were both hanged on a tree
11. If you were Mordecai would you have done or said anything or just acted like you knew nothing?
- Optional – their honest answer to this question lends its way for great discussions

Esther 3

1. The king's servants manipulated Haman much like instigators manipulate two people into fights. Explain
- They could not harm or punish Mordecai legally so they used Haman's arrogance, pride and anger weaknesses to manipulate him
- Instigators who dislike the same person you dislike will come up to you, remind you that you don't like the person, and tell you your mutual enemy said or did something against you. Beware of these kind of instigators
2. Was Haman angry with Mordecai before these servants spoke to him?
- No. It appears he had not noticed Mordecai prior
3. Should you beware of anyone coming to you and pointing out someone alleged to have disrespected you to your face repeatedly that you did not notice?
- Yes. If you hadn't noticed, then it obviously was not bothering you. Why would someone tell you something they know is going to upset you unless they wanted to bait you?
4. Why do you think these servants told Haman about Mordecai?
- To stir the pot and start trouble for Mordecai
- Because they did not like Mordecai
- Because they had a problem with Jews
5. Could these servants possibly be jealous and upset with Haman about his promotion?
- Yes. That is a definite possibility
6. Why was it important to note that when they found out Mordecai was a Jew the servants decided to report him?
- Because this was also a race issue
7. Now Haman noticed Mordecai didn't bow or reverence him and Haman was happy right?

- (5) Wrong. Haman was full of wrath. For Haman it wasn't good enough to punish just Mordecai, once finding out he was a Jew Haman wanted all Jews destroyed
8. Mordecai had been doing this and Haman was unaffected so it wasn't the event, what changed?
- His attention was now drawn to Mordecai with a negative perception along with it
- Haman lost his peace
9. How do you think the servants characterized Mordecai to Haman to get this new response?
- Are you going to let a Jew disrespect you like that in front of everyone?
- People are going to think you are a punk undeserving of your new promotion
- I guess it's true that you don't have the guts to hold the position the king gave you
10. Did Haman want to punish just Mordecai?
- (5, 6KJV/6NLT) No. His anger for Mordecai caused him to conspire to destroy all Jews
11. Haman's anger was magnification and escalating in what way?
- He took a small issue that he had not even noticed prior and blew it into a big issue
12. What did Haman recommend to the king because he was offended by Mordecai?
- (8KJV/8NLT) – pitch to the king to kill a race of people
13. If you not only suggest a plan but provide funding to legislate it does this make those in authority pay attention?
- (9) Yes
14. Was Haman known to have a good relationship with all races?
- (10) No. He was referred to as the Jews' enemy

15. When the king gave Haman his ring, was this a good move because he could trust Haman to act fairly?
- No. (10) the king gave the Jews enemy authority
16. Did the king give any special instruction to Haman not to abuse his authority?
- (11) No. He gave him power to do what he wanted
17. When if at all did Haman have an order written into law?
- (7) March 7
- (12KJV/12NLT) April 17 Haman had his order written into law
18. What was the consequence if any for defying the new law?
- (13KJV/13NLT) It decreed all Jews young and old including women and children must be killed on a single day
19. Was there a reward / incentive for reporting violators? If your answer is yes, what was it?
- (13KJV/13NLT) Yes. The violators property was given to those who killed them
20. Do you think offering a reward or incentive would inspire people who may not normally want to act?
- Yes.
21. Who if anyone would be punished?
- Jews
22. What had to happen before people were ready to act?
- (14) The word had to get out
23. Once the decree went out what was the king and Haman's reaction?
- (15) The king and Haman sat and drank together
24. What was the reaction of the people in the city?
- (15) The city of Shushan/Susa was confused

Esther 4

1. How did Mordecai react when he found out about the new law?
- (1) Mordecai found out and was angry (rent his clothes). He ran out into the street and cried out bitterly
2. Was Mordecai's dramatic response in compliance with their laws and customs?
- (2) Though angry he did not defy the law and protested legally – he stood outside the palace gate
3. If you act in compliance to a written law in your jurisdiction, is that enough to justify your actions? Explain
- No. Not all laws are just and moral, because it's written is not enough
- No. Midwives defied the written law to kill newborn Hebrews – Exodus 1:15-22
- Herod put out a law to kill all babies under the age of two – Matthew 2:16
- Darius was tricked into making a law to only worship him – Daniel 6:12-28
4. Was Mordecai's anger needless? Explain
- Optional – their honest answer to this question lends its way for great discussions
5. Was Mordecai's anger just? Explain
- Optional – their honest answer to this question lends its way for great discussions
6. Was Mordecai's anger causing a problem? Explain
- Optional – their honest answer to this question lends its way for great discussions
7. How did the Jews respond?
- (3) as word spread the Jews mourned, fasted, wept, wailed and many lay in sackcloth and ashes

8. Esther sent Mordecai clothing when she found out he was protesting. Was he grateful? Why or why not?
- (4) Queen Esther found out and sent clothes to Mordecai but he refused them. He was not grateful and wanted to make a statement
9. Did Esther send a messenger to arrest Mordecai and have him locked up?
- No
10. Where was Mordecai protesting? Why do you think he chose this location?
- In front of the king's gate
- He was sure to be noticed, seen and heard
11. Being seen and heard are character traits of what personality type?
- Funnies
12. Did the manner in which Mordecai chose to protest help or hurt his cause?
- Helped because it got Esther's attention and it was legal
13. Would you protest the same way Mordecai did if it were legal?
- Optional and variety of answers acceptable as long as they are honest
14. What is the point of protesting?
- Optional and variety of answers acceptable as long as they are honest
- To bring attention to your cause and make your voice heard loud and clear
15. How do you respond to authority figures and institutions when you feel their actions are adversely unfair?
- Optional and variety of answers acceptable as long as they are honest

16. Mordecai responded and answered the question what was wrong. He didn't just ask that his word be taken as proof, what else did Mordecai do that helped his position?
- (8) he gave the documentation as evidence and charged Esther to plead with the king for her people
17. Who did Mordecai ask and depend on to do something about the problem?
- Queen Esther
18. Should Mordecai have waited until he had organized a large group of supporters before acting?
- No. They were running out of time
19. If you were Esther would you jeopardize your life and status to jump into this fight? Why or why not?
- Optional and variety of answers acceptable as long as they are honest
20. Esther had a good reason not to approach the king, what was it?
- (11) Esther cited the law that she could not go into the king's inner court/domain without being summoned or called
21. Is it important to know the law when you want to fight something you perceive as an injustice? Explain
- Optional and variety of answers acceptable as long as they are honest
- Yes. Otherwise you can get shut down without being heard.
22. What arguments were given to Esther if she did nothing?
- (13) Mordecai replied, the Jews will be delivered if you (Esther) are silent, you and your family won't survive. You are in the palace likely to make a difference right now, just for this purpose
23. List some things trend setters, freedom fighters, and advocates must be willing to do to try to reverse injustice:
- Learn the law

- Form a plan
- Risk severe penalty – incarceration, fines, loss of income and livelihood, injury, and death
24. Is it important to have faith and a spiritual foundation to reflect on? Explain
- Optional and variety of answers acceptable as long as they are honest
25. What five words are Esther famous for saying regarding how much she was willing to sacrifice?
- (16) "If I perish, I perish"
26. What is Mordecai's famous saying to Esther regarding her purpose in life?
- (13) You are in the palace likely to make a difference right now, just for this purpose & "For such a time as this"
27. What did Esther ask Mordecai to do?
- (16) Esther said for Mordecai to get all Jews together in Shusham, and fast for her
28. Did Mordecai comply?
- (17) Yes
29. Often people ask you to take and put yourself at risk but are not willing to do anything themselves, true or false?
- True

Esther 5
1. Did Esther approach the king wisely or recklessly?
- wisely
2. Did the king have the same regard for Esther that he had for Queen Vashti? Explain
- (2) No. Esther obtained favor in his sight.
3. Was Queen Esther and Queen Vashti regarded by king Ahasuerus the same? Explain

- No. Vashti was disrespected and treated like a trophy and property. He respected and regarded Esther.
4. What promise did the king make to Queen Esther?
- (3) I'll give you anything to the half of my kingdom
5. When a king made a vow or public promise could he later change his mind? Explain
- No. Whatever a king decreed could not be reversed normally, not even by him.
6. What other stories in the Bible do you know of where kings made a law or promise and wished they had not?
- Optional and variety of answers acceptable as long as they are honest and explained
- Daniel – Darius (Daniel 6:12-18)
- John the Baptist – Herod (Matthew 14:7-9)
- David – Saul (1 Samuel 26:21)
- Moses – Rameses/Pharaoh (Exodus 4:22-23) & (Exodus 10:16-17)
7. How much was the king willing to grant Esther?
- Up to the half of his kingdom
8. King Ahasuerus' willingness to grant Esther whatever she wanted without knowing what she would ask for says what about his views and feelings for her?
- He trusted her
- He held her in high regard
- By law it was probably all he could offer her
9. Have you built the kind of relationship with your parents where you can garner the same response from them that the king gave Esther? Explain ways you can do this:
- Take care of your responsibilities
- Know and honor the household rules without having to be told repeatedly and reminded

- Approach your parents respectfully at the appropriate times
- Avoid requests that are self-serving and gear them more toward those of civic or community service
- Show your gratitude and appreciation for what your parents do for you each day
- Exercise being humble not arrogant when you ask your parents for things

10. The king obligated Haman to attend Esther's banquet, why?
- Simply because Esther requested his presence

11. Have you earned the kind of trust and respect the king had for Esther? Explain
- Optional and variety of answers acceptable as long as they are honest

12. Are your requests met with many questions to determine your agenda or what you are choosing not to tell your parents? Explain
- Optional and variety of answers acceptable as long as they are honest

13. Or are your parent's eager to give you any requests you make because you have lived a responsible honest life thus far? Explain
- Optional and variety of answers acceptable as long as they are honest

14. Are there changes you can make to rebuild trust and earn your parents respect? List them:
- Yes
- Optional and variety of answers acceptable as long as they are honest
- Follow their rules to the letter
- Don't knowingly cause them grief or embarrassment
- Be consistent doing your chores and fulfilling your responsibilities without needing them to remind you

- Have a good attitude and don't have a bad attitude
- Don't argue
- Apologize for bad behavior and do not repeat it
15. Have you ever let your parents down after they trusted you with permission to do something?
- Optional and variety of answers acceptable as long as they are honest
16. Was it a big deal for the king to be willing to grant Esther an unknown request? Explain
- Yes. Once he speaks it he must grant it so it's risky to give an open-ended promise like that
17. Have you taken your parent's permission for granted in the past? Will you correct that now?
- Optional and variety of answers acceptable as long as they are honest
18. Even after being granted anything she wished, Esther responded humble and gracious. Explain
- It shows the character Esther had and that the king's trust was warranted
19. Haman felt good about himself after receiving the invitation until what happened?
- (9) Haman felt good until he saw Mordecai then he lost his joy and glad heart because Mordecai didn't stand up for Haman at the king's gate
20. Was Haman's anger needless? Explain
- Optional and variety of answers acceptable as long as they are honest
21. Was Haman's anger just? Explain
- Optional and variety of answers acceptable as long as they are honest
22. Did the act/event justify the level of Haman's anger? Explain
- No

- It was a small gesture that he should have let go immediately
- Because Haman felt disrespected, he wanted to have an entire race of people killed

23. What did Haman decide to do about his anger? Why?

- (9) Haman was furious at Mordecai not being intimidated by him
- (10) for a more pleasant anticipated experience he brushed off his discontent for Mordecai and went on to notify his wife and friends about the banquet

24. Was Haman a humble guy? Explain

- (10-11) No. He went home and quickly gathered his friends and his wife together so he could boast

25. Did Haman have anything to be thankful for?

- (11) in pride Haman bragged and boasted about his wealth, promotion, family being above the princes and servants of the king

26. With all that Haman had, how did he let his anger cause him to focus on an encounter that upset him?

- He was stuck in "past anger" patterns and allowing an incident in his past dictate his mood and bad behavior in the present

27. When Haman was boasting do you think this was helping him win friends or causing people to be jealous of him and not like him?

- (12) Haman went on to say he was the only one invited to the banquet with the king and had another invitation to be with the royals the next/following day
- This is likely to cause others to be envious and not like him

28. Do jealous people wait for an opportunity to bring you down or lift you up?

- They typically try to bring you down at any given opportunity

29. Have you ever had an experience with a jealous person who was upset with you? Tell me about it
- Optional and variety of answers acceptable as long as they are honest
30. What was Haman's wife's name?
- Zeresh
31. Haman's wife suggested Haman ask the king for permission to hang Mordecai. Does she sound like a good person to be around and influencing Haman?
- No
32. Who have you been around who is like Haman's wife?
- Optional and variety of answers acceptable as long as they are honest
33. What did Haman think of his wife's idea?
- (14) He thought this sounded like a great idea. He took the next step and had the gallows prepared

Esther 6
1. When the king could not sleep what did he decide to do?
- (1) he had the book of records of the chronicles brought and read to him
2. When you are bored and can't sleep what do you do with your time?
- Optional and variety of answers acceptable as long as they are honest
3. What did the king uncover?
- (2) he found out Mordecai was the whistleblower who exposed the assassination attempt against him (king Ahasuerus)
4. Was the king angry after finding out this new information? If not, what was his response?
- (3) No. He wanted to be sure Mordecai was rewarded

5. Who did the king uncover information about?
- (2-3) Mordecai
6. Who showed up in the king's outward court?
- (4) Haman
7. What did this person want?
- (4) to ask that Mordecai be hanged
8. What did the king ask Haman's opinion on?
- (6) the king asked Haman what can be done to honor a man I delight in
9. Did Haman give the king good advice?
- (7-9) Yes. It was over the top
10. Why do you think he gave the advice he did?
- (6) because Haman thought he was the person the king wanted to honor
11. Did the king like Haman's ideas? How do you know?
- Yes
- (10) the king told Haman to do all he said for Mordecai the Jew that sits at the king's gate. Do all you suggested without fail
12. Although the king told Haman to carry out his ideas, was Haman happy to do it? Explain
- Optional and variety of answers acceptable as long as they are honest
- No
- (6) Haman had only made such an extravagant suggestion because he thought the honor and display would be for him
- This is also a reminder that just because someone does something for you does not mean their heart is in it
13. True or false, Haman did as the king instructed?
- (11) True
14. This time when Mordecai went to the king's gate, what did Haman do?

- (12) this time Haman rushed home dejected and humiliated
15. Was Haman a prejudice racist? Explain
- Optional and variety of answers acceptable as long as they are honest
16. Did Haman speak highly of Mordecai to others? Explain
- Optional and variety of answers acceptable as long as they are honest
- (13) No. His wife and friends knew Mordecai was an enemy of Haman's who Haman despised and wanted eliminated
17. What advice was Haman given regarding whether or not to pursue action against Mordecai?
- (13) Haman told his wife and all his friends what happened and they said because Mordecai is a Jew who humiliated you, you'll never be able to carry out your plans against him. It would be a fatal mistake to keep opposing Mordecai
18. What happened next to insure Haman made it to Esther's banquet?
- (14) Just then the king's chamberlains arrived to take Haman to the banquet Esther prepared

Esther 7
1. What 3 primary guests were at the banquet?
- (1) King Ahasuerus, Queen Esther and Haman
2. Did the king vow again for the third time that he would give Esther anything she wanted?
- (2) Yes. The king yet again on the second day of the banquet vowed to grant Esther anything to the half of the kingdom
3. Was there a limit?
- (2) Yes. Anything to the half of the kingdom
4. Did Esther finally reveal what she wanted of the king?
- (3) Yes

5. What did she request?
- (3) Esther asked in humility, "If I'm worthy please spare my life and the lives of my people"
6. What was Esther's attitude like when she made the request?
- humbled
7. Esther said she would not have made a request if the circumstances were different. Explain.
- (4) She said, "We've been sold to people planning to kill, slaughter and annihilate us. If we had been sold to be slaves I wouldn't bother the king with such a matter of business"
8. Was Esther's request urgent? Explain.
- Optional and variety of answers acceptable as long as they are honest
- Yes
- Esther and her people's lives and freedom were in immediate jeopardy. Time was of the essence as Haman had hatched a plan that was already in the works.
9. Did the king see Esther's request as urgent? How do you know?
- Yes
- (5) King Ahasuerus asked Esther who would do such a thing and be so heartless
10. How did the king characterize the person responsible for Esther's dilemma?
- (5) heartless
11. When the king asked who was to blame for Esther's problem, who did she name?
- (6) Haman
12. How did Esther characterize the person she blamed?
- (6) the enemy is this wicked Haman
13. When Esther named the perpetrator who caused her problem how did the king react?

- (7) The king jumped up in rage
14. What was a positive act made in this chapter to control rage?
- (7) The king went out into the palace garden
15. When the problem person was exposed, did this person do anything to make matters better or worse? Explain
- (7-8) Worse. Haman stayed behind to plead for his life with Queen Esther because he knew he was in trouble with the king and there was no way out. In despair Haman fell upon the bed/couch where Esther was reclining and the king returned into the room and said to Haman, "Will you assault the queen right here in the palace in front of me?"
16. What did the king's attendants do that signaled the culprit's fate?
- (8) the king's attendants covered Haman's face
17. Name the chamberlain who told the king about the gallows the person built?
- Harbonah
18. How high was this gallows?
- (9) fifty cubits (75 feet) high
19. Where was the gallows located?
- (9) in his (Haman's) own courtyard
20. Who do you know that is like this informant?
- Optional and variety of answers acceptable as long as they are honest
21. What instigators have you known to watch someone hatch a vicious plot, and say or do nothing to try to talk sense into the person. Yet when the person got found out and was now in trouble the instigators tell all they know against the person?
- Optional and variety of answers acceptable as long as they are honest

22. Do you think the informant was thought of as a friend by the perpetrator? Explain
- Yes. How else would he have had this information if he were not in Haman's circle of friends that he confided in?
23. Who was planned to be hanged on the gallows?
- (10) Mordecai
24. Who ended up being hanged on the gallows?
- (10) Haman
25. Did this informant say anything that instigated the perpetrator's penalty?
- (9) Yes
26. What did the informant say that made him look like an evil instigator?
- (9) King, Haman had gallows built to hang Mordecai, the man who spoke good of you king and saved you from assassination
27. Should you be careful of people like this informant who are quick to switch sides and throw others under the bus rather quickly? Do you know anyone who does this?
- Yes
- Optional and variety of answers acceptable as long as they are honest
28. Do you hang around any people who hear you hatching an evil plot and act like they are in support of it, but when it goes bad then tell you how you never should have contemplated such poor decisions?
- Optional and variety of answers acceptable as long as they are honest
29. List 5 people that you call your friends, and list the reasons you consider them friends:
- Optional – their honest answer to this question lends its way for great discussions

- 1__________________________________
- 2__________________________________
- 3__________________________________
- 4__________________________________
- 5__________________________________

30. After the culprit was hanged what happened to the king's anger?
- (10) the king's wrath/anger was pacified
31. Is it important for a leader or authority figure to have control over their anger? Explain
- Yes. They have greater responsibility and are in charge of people under their control

Esther 8
1. What is the significance in who and how Mordecai met king Ahasuerus?
- (1) Esther introduced Mordecai and told the king who Mordecai was to Esther
2. When you do not introduce someone you claim to love or respect to your family, what do you think your family is left to conclude about how much you care about the person?
- They believe you do not love or regard the other person and that's why you haven't introduced them to the truly important people in your life
3. What ended up happening to Haman's house?
- (1) King Ahasuerus gave Haman's house to Esther

4. What did the king take back from Haman and give Mordecai?
- (2) ring
5. What scripture in Proverbs chapter 13 addresses what happens to the wealth of sinners?
- Verse 22
- *A good man leaveth an inheritance to his children's children: and the wealth of the sinner is laid up for the just. KJV*
6. When Esther made her request to the king, did it seem unimportant to her? Explain
- (3) No. It was important to her
- (3) Esther again begged the king with tears and fell at his feet to put away Haman's mischief devised against the Jews
7. What did she plead with the king to do?
- (4-5) write a reversal letter to the one Haman wrote to destroy the Jews, and distribute it out in all the king's provinces
8. How did the king respond?
- (8) He gave Esther the authority to write a reversal however she chose in his (the king's) name, sealed with his ring and it would be unable to be reversed
9. How much did the king trust Esther? Explain
- (8) Explicitly. He gave Esther the authority to write a reversal in his name with no restrictions, and told her how to do so to avoid it being reversed
10. Can your parents trust you like king Ahasuerus trusted Esther?
- Optional and variety of answers acceptable as long as they are honest
11. What did Haman's letter say was to happen?
- (5) destroy the Jews in all the king's provinces

12. Are there people like Haman still in positions of authority today?
- Optional – their honest answer to this question lends its way for great discussions
13. Have you encountered someone who is in a powerful position who has some of the same beliefs as Haman?
- Optional – their honest answer to this question lends its way for great discussions
14. Is it dangerous to give someone like Haman power? Explain
- Optional – their honest answer to this question lends its way for great discussions
15. If you were Haman's boss, would you want to be responsible for the things he does when you are not looking?
- No
16. Did you know that parents are less likely to give their children permission and liberties when their youth betray their trust, commit an illegal act, behave irresponsibly or lie to them?
- Optional – their honest answer to this question lends its way for great discussions
17. Have you done anything that would cause your parents to be hesitant to trust you?
- Optional – their honest answer to this question lends its way for great discussions
18. When you continue to ask for privileges when you never showed remorse or repentance for prior privileges extended to you that you disregarded and were unappreciative of, why would your parents give you more?
- Optional – their honest answer to this question lends its way for great discussions
19. Did Esther like to see people hurt and destroyed? Explain
- No

- (6) she could not bear to see the evil and destruction of her people/kindred
20. Why did king Ahasuerus say Haman was hanged?
- (7) because he laid his hands upon the Jews
21. What did the king give Esther the ability to do?
- (8) He gave Esther the authority to write a reversal however she chose in his (the king's) name, sealed with his ring and it would be unable to be reversed
22. Is this because whatever Esther decided was a decision that would only be in effect 48 hours? Explain
- No
- (8) if done properly it could not be reversed
23. How much discretion did the king give Esther?
- (8) complete
24. The king also told Esther what to do so her decision would not be amended, what was this?
- (8) She could use his (the king's) name, seal the writing with his ring and it would be unable to be reversed
25. What does this say about how the king felt about Esther?
- He trusted, regarded and loved her
26. The king had already been betrayed by Haman, and felt disrespected by Queen Vashti, is this good reasons not to ever trust anyone ever again?
- No
27. Which of the four personality types gives people more chances than they deserve and is more likely to allow themselves to be betrayed more than the other 3 personality types?
- Heartthrob
28. Have you ever had people close to you betray you or let you down? Explain

- Optional – their honest answer to this question lends its way for great discussions
29. Do you think this gives you good reason not to trust anyone ever again?
- No. We should continue to trust but not continue to trust those who have shown themselves unworthy. Let them earn it back if they really want it.
30. Who was given permission to dictate a decree to the king's scribes?
- (9) Mordecai
31. Who was the decree sent out to and why?
- (9) to the Jews, princes, governors and local officials of all 127 provinces from India to Ethiopia
- He had to make those subject to it, and those who would be enforcing it, aware of it before it could be enacted
32. Which language(s) was the script(s) sent out in?
- (9) languages of all the people of the empire including the Jews
33. Is there a reason why they didn't just make a verbal announcement to the people?
- Yes. Laws and policies must be in writing for clarity, documentation and future reference
34. List all the rules that were followed to attempt to reverse Haman's decree?
- Optional and variety of answers acceptable as long as they are honest
- Notification must be made to the people in all languages
- The reversal decree must be written in writing
- The king had to be told and be in agreement
- Authority to use the king's name had to be given
- Authority extended to use the kings ring to seal the decree

35. What unique privilege did the reversal decree grant the Jews?

- (11) It gave the Jews of any and every city authority and the right to defend their lives. They could kill, slaughter and annihilate anyone of any nationality or province who might assault them, their children or their wives, and they could take the property of their enemies

36. What day was chosen for this event?

- (12) the thirteenth day of the twelfth month, which is the month Adar – March 7 the next year

37. What needed to happen next?

- (13) The copy of the writing for a commandment had to be given / published to everyone in every province

38. What did the Jews need to be ready that day to do?

- (13) avenge themselves on their enemies

39. What did the posts / messengers go out on?

- (14) mules, camels, horses

40. Did these posts / messengers take their time doing the king's service?

- (14) No. They were swift feeling pressured by the king's command

41. Where was it said the decree was given at?

- (14) Shushan the palace

42. When Mordecai stepped out in royal apparel how did the city react?

- (15) the city rejoiced and was glad

43. Find the scripture in Proverbs 29 that makes reference to the type of reaction the people gave Mordecai.

- *Proverbs 29:2 KJV – When the righteous are in authority, the people rejoice: but when the wicked beareth rule, the people mourn*

44. Why do you think the Jews were especially happy to see Mordecai in such a high position?
- (16) It gave the Jews light, joy, gladness and honor
45. Is there anyone you have seen succeed that gave you hope that you could attain what prior to that seemed impossible?
- Optional – their honest answer to this question lends its way for great discussions
46. What did people who were not Jews decide to do out of fear?
- (17) Many became Jews fearing what the Jews might do to them
47. Do you know of other circumstances or times when people adopted the traits of another culture to fit in and be relevant with the times?
- Optional and variety of answers acceptable as long as they are honest
- Rachel Dolezal – NAACP – 2017
- Iron Eyes Cody – crying Indian chief – 1904-1999
- William Lee Tipton (born Dorothy Lucille Tipton) – entertainer – 1914-1989
48. Have you ever felt the need to deny yourself or masquerade as someone other than your authentic self? Explain
- Optional – their honest answer to this question lends its way for great discussions

Esther 9

1. On what date did the two decrees go into effect?
- (1) On March 7 the two decrees were put into effect
2. On this date did the enemies of the Jews get what they hoped for? Explain
- No

- (2) The Jews organized and were ready for anyone seeking to harm them. They instilled fear into their enemies.
3. Did the Jews randomly start killing people or go on a killing spree? Explain
- No
- (5) the Jews struck down all their enemies and did what they wanted to those who hated them
4. Were these enemies still comfortable and open about their hatred and contempt for Jews? Explain
- No. The Jews organized and were ready for anyone seeking to harm them. They instilled fear into their enemies.
5. Were only the citizens in compliance with the decree?
- (3) No, all rulers of the provinces, lieutenants, deputies and officers of the king, helped the Jews fearing Mordecai
6. What others helped the Jews? Why?
- (3) All the rulers of the provinces, the lieutenants, the deputies and officers of the king, helped the Jews
- (3) The fear of Mordecai fell upon them
7. What kind of reputation if any did Mordecai have?
- (4) Mordecai was great in the king's house
8. Was Mordecai soon forgotten about?
- (4) No, his fame went throughout all provinces for he became more powerful
9. If Mordecai had tried to take this problem on himself early on and been a violent vigilante do you think he would have accomplished the same result? Explain
- No. They would have had reason to label him as violent, criminal, a threat to public safety and arrest or kill him
10. What were the Jews permitted to do to their enemies?
- (5) strike down all their enemies and do whatever they wanted to those who hated them
11. How many of Haman's sons were affected?

- (10) all 10
12. What happened to Haman's sons?
- Haman's 10 sons were killed
13. Did the king ever go to Esther and tell her he made a mistake giving her authority and was putting a stop to the decree she issued? Explain
- (12) No. He gave her an update of the death toll
14. What did the king ask Esther?
- (12) if she wanted anything else that it would be done
15. What was Esther's reply?
- (13) Esther asked again with humility to continue the decree another day and hang the bodies of Haman's 10 sons upon the gallows
16. Was Esther's attitude different now that she had power and her decree had been carried out? Explain
- (13) No. She still spoke to the king respectfully and with humility
17. If the king granted Esther's request, what was the outcome?
- (14) the Jews gathered again and slew 300 men
18. What happened to the prey/plunder?
- (14) They laid no hands on the prey/plunder
19. The other Jews who gathered were unable to come together and ended up killing each other, true or false?
- False
- (16) Other Jews gathered to defend their lives and slew 75,000 and took no plunder/prey
20. What did people do March 8?
- (17) March 8 they rested, and celebrated their victory
21. What did the Jews at Susa do on the 2nd and 3rd days?
- (18) the Jews at Susa continued killing their enemies on the 13th & 14th day – 2nd day then rested on the 15th/3rd day and made it a day of rest/fasting and gladness

22. Describe the demeanor of the Jews of the villages in unwalled towns:
- (19) The Jews of the villages in unwalled towns rejoiced and gave gifts
23. Why do you think Mordecai did what he did in verse 20?
- Optional – their honest answer to this question lends its way for great discussions
- Documentation is important for those in authority
24. What were the people encouraged to do in the future on these two days? Why?
- (21) to have an annual celebration those 2 days
- (22) to remember them as days the Jews rested from their enemies, turned their sorrow to joy, from mourning into a good day
- (22) to make these days of feasting and joy, and of sending gifts to each other and to the poor
25. Were the Jews receptive to Mordecai's suggestion? What did they do?
- (23) Yes
- the Jews adopted Mordecai's suggestion and began this annual custom
26. In your own words, list the events that were recommended the Jews commemorate:
- (24-25) Haman had plotted to have the Jews destroyed by casting lots (purim). Esther valiantly went before the king on the Jews' behalf. As a result, the king ordered a written decree that blocked Haman's wicked plan. Haman was outwitted and the scheme he had conjured up against the Jews backfired on his own head. Haman and his sons were hanged in the gallows
27. What did they call these days?
- (26) They call these days Purim after the name Pur

28. What did the Jews agree to do without fail?
- (27) The Jews agreed to inaugurate this tradition and pass it on to their descendants and those who became Jews. They vowed to never fail to celebrate these two days at the appointed time each year
29. How often were they going to celebrate?
- (27) Two days at the appointed time each year
30. What days are important to you each year?
- Optional – their honest answer to this question lends its way for great discussions
31. Do you celebrate them? Why? What significance do they have?
- Optional – their honest answer to this question lends its way for great discussions
32. Who did they want these important days to be remembered by?
- (28) every generation, every family, every province, and every city, among the Jews, and their seed
33. What two people wrote another letter?
- (29) Queen Esther & Mordecai wrote another letter
34. What was this letter supposed to do?
- (29) put the queen's full authority behind Mordecai's letter to establish the Festival of Purim/second letter of Purim
35. Where were the letters sent?
- (30) The letters were sent to the 127 provinces
36. What two things did the letter also have words of?
- (30) peace and truth/security
37. What did the letters confirm and/or establish?
- (31) These letters established / confirmed those days of Purim according as Mordecai and Queen Esther decreed for themselves and their descendants
38. What happened to Esther's decree?

- (32) Esther's decree was confirmed and written in the record book

Esther 10
1. Where were all Mordecai's acts written?
- (2) all acts of Mordecai's greatness are written in the book of the chronicles of the kings of Media and Persia
2. Was Mordecai given a lower position or high position? Explain
- (3) High position
- (3) Mordecai the Jew became prime minister/next unto king Ahasuerus with authority.
3. Was Mordecai despised or revered? Explain why
- (3) revered
- (3) He was great among the Jews who held him in high esteem because he worked for the good of his people, and sought wealth for his people
- (3) He was a friend of the royal court of all of them and spoke peace to all his seed

NOTES

SUGGESTIONS

If you are so overwhelmed with not knowing where to start in your journey to grow in the scriptures, you are not alone. Please avoid stressing yourself out to the point that you do nothing. Choose to *do something*! Even if that something that you do is as simple as opening The Bible and reading that page. The fantastic thing is you can never go wrong reading and studying any part of the word of God.

So shall my word be that goeth forth out of my mouth: it shall not return unto me void, but it shall accomplish that which I please, and it shall prosper in the thing whereto I sent it.
Isaiah 55:11 KJV

If my book has been a blessing to you, I invite you to continue studying the scriptures with me. Albeit, there are a multitude of alternatives to continue your search for answers. Below are some suggested options that I have heard over the years have helped give seekers of truth a nice place to begin:

1. The 10 Commandments
- Memorize and get to know these commandments as well as

you know your own address, birthdate, and phone numbers
- ***Exodus 20:1-17***

2. Proverbs
- There are a total of 31 chapters. Read a chapter each day for at least a year. Select at least one verse to meditate on for the whole day.
- ***Proverbs 1-31***

3. Ministry
- Locate and participate in a bible believing local church that has an active youth ministry and bible studies to help both you and your youth grow in the word.
- ***Hebrews 10:25***
    - *Not forsaking the assembling of ourselves together, as the manner of some is; but exhorting one another: and so much the more, as ye see the day approaching.*   *(KJV)*
    - *And let us not neglect our meeting together, as some people do, but encourage and warn each other, especially now that the day of his coming back again is drawing near.*   *(NLT)*

4. The 4 Gospels – Matthew, Mark, Luke & John
- Do not just read, study the life of Jesus through the eyes of four of his disciples.
- How did Christ talk and relate to people?
- What made him angry?
- The parables and stories he told, explain their significance.
- ***Mathew 1-28; Mark 1-16; Luke 1-24; John 1-21***

5. 1 Corinthians 13 – Charity/Love Chapter
- Based on this chapter, what is charity and how is it expressed?
- ***1 Corinthians 13:1-13***

6. Hebrews 11 – Heroes of faith
- Who were the heroes of faith?
- What were they able to accomplish by faith?
- ***Hebrews 11:1-40***

7. The 2 Greatest Commandments
- When Jesus was asked which of the commandments was greatest, what did He say?
- Jesus summed up the just of the scriptures into two commandments, they are vital to living a righteous life.
- ***Matthew 22:35-40 and Mark 12:28-34***

Matthew 22:37-40 KJV
- o *(37) Jesus said unto him, Thou shalt love the Lord thy God with all thy heart, and with all thy soul, and with all thy mind.*
- o *(38) This is the first and great commandment.*
- o *(39) And the second is like unto it, Thou shalt love thy neighbor as thyself.*
- o *(40) On these two commandments hang all the law and the prophets.*

Mark 12:30-31 KJV
- o *(30) And thou shalt love the Lord thy God with all thy heart, and with all thy soul, and with all thy mind, and with all thy strength: this is the first commandment.*

- o   *(31) And the second is like, namely this, Thou shalt love thy neighbor as thyself. There is none other commandment greater than these.*

The important thing is that you delve into the word, the manner in which you choose to do this is not as significant.

Avoid merely going through The Bible and *grow* through it!

HELPFUL SCRIPTURES

And if it seem evil unto you to serve the Lord, choose you this day whom ye will serve; whether the gods which your fathers served that were on the other side of the flood, or the gods of the Amorites, in whose land ye dwell: but as for me and my house, we will serve the Lord.
Joshua 24:15 KJV

Why should you study the scriptures?

All scripture is given by inspiration of God, and is profitable for doctrine, for reproof, for correction, for instruction in righteousness. **2 Timothy 3:16 KJV**

(20) Knowing this first, that no prophecy of the scripture is of any private interpretation. (21) For the prophecy came not in old time by the will of man: but holy men of God spake as they were moved by the Holy Ghost. **2 Peter 1:20-21 KJV**

Search the scriptures; for in them ye think ye have eternal life: and they are they which testify of me. **John 5:39 KJV**

Sanctify them through thy truth: thy word is thy truth
John 17:17 KJV

So we must listen very carefully to the truth we have heard, or we may drift away from it. **Hebrews 2:1 NLT**

Who is wise, and he shall understand these things? Prudent, and he shall know them? For the ways of the Lord are right, and the just shall walk in them: but the transgressors shall fall therein. **Hosea 14:9 KJV**
And be not conformed to this world: but be ye transformed by the renewing of your mind, that ye may prove what is that good, and acceptable, and perfect, will of God. **Romans 12:2 KJV**

When at your wits end, find hope in this:
(30) Even the youths shall faint and be weary, and the young men shall utterly fall: (31) But they that wait upon the Lord shall renew their strength; they shall mount up with wings as eagles; they shall run, and not be weary; and they shall walk, and not faint. **Isaiah 40:28-31 KJV**
He shall not be afraid of evil tidings: his heart is fixed, trusting in the Lord. **Psalm 112:7 KJV**
In all labour there is profit: but the talk of the lips tendeth only to penury. **Proverbs 14:23 KJV**
And let us not be weary in well doing: for in due season we shall reap, if ye faint not. **Galatians 6:9 KJV**

Let God & His word be the ultimate source:
For we are the circumcision, which worship God in the spirit, and rejoice in Christ Jesus, and have no confidence in the flesh.
Philippians 3:3 KJV
For the commandment is a lamp; and the law is light; and reproofs of instruction are the way of life:
Proverbs 6:23 KJV
(5) Trust in the Lord with all thine heart; and lean not unto thine own understanding. (6) In all thy ways acknowledge him, and he shall direct thy paths. (7) Be not wise in thine own eyes: fear the Lord, and depart from evil. **Proverbs 3:5-7 KJV**

Then he answered and spake unto me, saying, This is the word of the Lord unto Zerubbabel, saying, Not by might, nor by power, but by my spirit, saith the Lord of hosts.   **Zechariah 4:6 KJV**

Be on one accord without fighting:
(2) Fulfil ye my joy, that ye be likeminded, having the same love, being of one accord, of one mind. (3) Let nothing be done through strife or vainglory; but in lowliness of mind let each esteem other better than themselves.
(12) Wherefore, my beloved, as ye have always obeyed, not as in my presence only, but now much more in my absence, work out your own salvation with fear and trembling. (13) For it is God which worketh in you both to will and to do of his good pleasure. (14) Do all things without murmurings and disputings. (15) That ye may be blameless and harmless, the sons of God, without rebuke, in the midst of a crooked and perverse nation, among whom ye shine as lights in the world.
(21) For all seek their own, not the things which are Jesus Christ's.   **Philippians 2:2-3, 12-15, 21 KJV**
I hope all of you who are mature Christians will agree on these things. If you disagree on some point, I believe God will make it plain to you.   **Philippians 3:15 NLT**

How to get a move from God:
If my people, which are called by my name, shall humble themselves, and pray, and seek my face, and turn from their wicked ways; then will I hear from heaven, and will forgive their sin, and will heal their land.   **2 Chronicles 7:14 KJV**

For where two or three are gathered together in my name, there am I in the midst of them.   **Matthew 18:20 KJV**

LETTER FROM THE AUTHOR

Parents you have the toughest job ever. I am certain you criticize and browbeat yourself, and agonize over the best way to raise your children. The greatest hope you have is to dig into the word of God and let the Holy Spirit reveal how to nurture and cultivate a positive relationship with your youth.

There is nothing new under the sun. Any good advice is undeniably a piggyback of a biblical standard. Lately, I have heard of Vision Boards being endorsed for those striving to achieve personal goals or business ventures. This is not an original concept.

Also, successful businesspeople recommend that upcoming entrepreneurs upgrade their self-talk and appearance. The advice is, "Represent yourself not just where you are but dress, speak and look the part of the job and position you desire to have." Again, this is great information but not unique.

Two scriptures immediately come to mind that have promoted these two same principles.

And the Lord answered me, and said, Write the vision, and make it plain upon tables, that he may run that readeth it.
Habakkuk 2:2 KJV
That is what the Scriptures mean when God told him, "I have made you the father of many nations," This happened because Abraham believed in the God who brings the dead back to life and who brings into existence what didn't exist before.
Romans 4:17 NLT

Habakkuk reminds us to put our aspirations in writing and on paper so we can envision them and pursue them with passion. Romans lets us know we should speak things not yet manifested into existence by *calling those things which are not as though they are.*

Rest assured if there is wisdom to be found about anything, it was first provided in the scriptures.

I am warning you ahead of time, dear friends, so that you can watch out and not be carried away by the errors of these wicked people. I don't want you to lose your own secure footing.
2 Peter 3:17 NLT

The world constantly changes the rules and lowers the bar to satisfy man's lust and selfish desires. God's standards raise the bar to cause us to be of service to others and glorify God.

(32) Now therefore hearken unto me, O ye children: for blessed are they that keep my ways.
(33) Hear instruction, and be wise, and refuse it not.
Proverbs 8:32-33

The greatest book ever written is the Holy Bible. You will never find a more influential piece of literature in the world. I strongly recommend this as being the final authority and ultimate reference for righteous living.

Adults and teens, be encouraged!

*   *   *

If you would like to send me a message or to acquire other resources of mine, you may contact me at TBillBooks@yahoo.com. Please no attachments or the email will be spammed.

In order to answer the anger and personality type questions in my books, please sign up and enroll in two of my preliminary online courses if you have not already done so:

Anger Management
https://rental-match-academy.thinkific.com/courses/anger-management2

4 Personality Types
https://rental-match-academy.thinkific.com/courses/4-personality-types

PRAYER OF SALVATION

How do you get saved? What is the prayer of salvation? What words do you say?

I do not pretend to speak for God. Many will say you must be in a church, or accept Christ publicly in front of others for it to count. Some say you must be baptized a specific way. I say, what does The Bible say about how to attain salvation?

For God so loved the world, that he gave his only begotten Son, that whosoever believeth in him should not perish, but have everlasting life. **John 3:16 KJV**

(9) That if thou shalt confess with thy mouth the Lord Jesus, and shalt believe in thine heart that God hath raised him from the dead, thou shalt be saved.
(10) For with the heart man believeth unto righteousness; and with the mouth confession is made unto salvation.
Romans 10:9-10 KJV

(9) I am the door: by me if any man enter in, he shall be saved, and shall go in and out, and find pasture.
(10) The thief cometh not, but for to steal and to kill, and to destroy: I am come that they might have life, and that they might have it more abundantly.

John 10:9-10 KJV

Jesus saith unto him, I am the way, the truth, and the life: no man cometh unto the Father, but by me.

John 14:6 KJV

(10) Be it known unto you all, and to all the people of Israel, that by the name of Jesus Christ of Nazareth, whom ye crucified, whom God raised from the dead, even by him doth this man stand here before you whole.
(11) This is the stone which was set at nought of you builders, which is become the head of the corner.
(12) Neither is there salvation in any other: for there is none other name under heaven given among men, whereby we must be saved.

Acts 4:10-12 KJV

Based on these scriptures the qualifiers are:
- I must know and acknowledge **JESUS** is the only way to God
- I must BELIEVE in Christ Jesus (Son of God)
- I must CONFESS Jesus with my mouth and BELIEVE in my heart God raised him from the dead